ideas

ideas

spaces
espacios
espaces
räume

AUTHORS
Fernando de Haro & Omar Fuentes

EDITORIAL DESIGN & PRODUCTION

ARQUITECTOS EDITORES MEXICANOS

PROJECT MANAGER
Valeria Degregorio Vega
Tzacil Cervantes Ortega

COORDINATION
Susana Madrigal Gutiérrez

COPYWRITER
Roxana Villalobos

ENGLISH TRANSLATION
Mexidiom Traducciones

FRENCH & GERMAN TRANSLATION
Tr@duce

Ideas
spaces · espacios · espaces · räume

© 2005, Fernando de Haro & Omar Fuentes

AM Editores S.A. de C.V.
Paseo de Tamarindos 400 B, suite 102, Col. Bosques de las Lomas,
C.P. 05120, México, D.F. Tels. 52(55) 5258 0279, Fax. 52(55) 5258 0556.
E-mail: ame@ameditores.com   www.ameditores.com

ISBN 970 - 9726 - 13 - 7

INDEX • INDICE

introduction • introducción • Introdiction • einleitung   8

introduction   introducción

IMAGE is always the starting point for the development of spaces for work, sales and services.

Although it may seem simple, making a particular image part of the identity of a specific space is no small feat, because the design requires a sharp focus on how to create a stimulus that impacts and captures the client's attention, and which also accurately conveys the profile of the company while attempting to maintain a holistic decorative vision.

YA SEA que se trate de un corporativo, de un producto o de un servicio la imagen es siempre el punto de partida para el desarrollo del diseño de lugares para el trabajo, comerciales y de servicios.

Aunque parece sencillo, en realidad hacer que se materialice una imagen determinada como parte de la identidad en un espacio específico no es cosa fácil, pues el diseño requiere de un enfoque muy preciso en el que ante todo se considere la manera

introduction   einleitung

QU'IL S'AGISSE d'un siège social, d'un produit ou d'un service, l'image est toujours le point de départ du développement de lieux de travail, commerciaux ou de services.

Bien que cela semble simple, faire en sorte de matérialiser une image déterminée pour qu'elle fasse partie de l'identité d'un espace spécifique n'est en réalité pas facile, puisque le design requière d'une orientation très précise selon laquelle on doit

EGAL ob es sich um eine Körperschaft handelt, um ein Produkt oder um eine Dienstleistung, das Image ist immer der Ausgangspunkt für den Entwurf von Arbeits-, Geschäfts- und Dienstleistungsräumen.

Auch wenn es einfach scheint, ist das Materalisieren eines bestimmten Image, als Bestandteil der Identität eines spezifischen Raumes, keine so leichte Sache, da der Entwurf eine sehr genaue Zielstellung verlangt, bei der vor allem die Art betrachtet wird, auf die Anreize

Therefore, to complete this kind of project, one must first perform a thorough assessment of the physical space and define the proper philosophy and image for each particular case. It is also necessary to understand the importance of interdisciplinary design work, given that the participation of different specialists will be required to fully develop and complete the project.

The shape and sequences of the space influence the composition of the image, given that the mechanics of volume are as important as the traffic schemes; the hierarchy given to the different areas; the layout, type, systems and dimension of the furniture incorporated into the space; the materials and finishes of surfaces; the color of the walls, furniture and accessories; the criteria used in the combination of different lighting techniques and levels; fixtures in general; as well as the layout of all these elements and the way in which they interact.

atención del cliente, transmitiéndole con precisión el perfil de la empresa y al mismo tiempo cuidando que se mantenga una visión unitaria en la decoración.

Por esta razón, para realizar un proyecto de este tipo lo primero que se demanda es efectuar un análisis completo del lugar, adentrarse en la filosofía e imagen adecuada de cada caso y comprender la importancia que tiene el trabajo de diseño interdisciplinario, pues se requerirá de la intervención de distintos especialistas para concluir el proyecto con un buen desarrollo.

Influyen en la conformación de la imagen la forma y las secuencias del espacio, dado que la mecánica de los volúmenes es tan importante como los esquemas de circulación; la jerarquía que se dé a las diversas zonas; la distribución, tipo, sistemas y dimensión del mobiliario que se integre; los materiales y el acabado que

avant tout considérer comment créer des stimulus qui impactent et captent l'attention du client, en lui transmettant avec précision le profil de l'entreprise et en soignant en même temps une vision homogène dans la décoration.

Afin de réaliser un tel projet, la première chose à faire est l'analyse complète de l'endroit physique, se concentrer ensuite sur la philosophie et l'image adéquate pour chaque cas particulier et saisir l'importance du travail de conception interdisciplinaire, puisque l'intervention de différents spécialistes est nécessaire pour concevoir un bon projet de développement.

Dans la création d'une image, sont importants la forme et l'enchaînement de l'espace, étant donné que la mécanique des volumes est aussi importante que les schémas de circulation ; la hiérarchie des

zu schaffen sind, die die Aufmerksamkeit des Kunden erwecken und fesseln, wobei das Firmenprofil deutlich wird und man zugleich die einheitliche Vision der Innenausstattung bewahrt.

Aus diesem Grund ist zur Durchführung eines solchen Projekts zuerst eine vollständige Analyse der örtlichen Gegebenheiten wichtig, wobei die geeignete Philosophie und das Image eines jeden Falles untersucht werden und die Bedeutung der interdisziplinären Entwurfsarbeit klar wird, da die Mitwirkung verschiedener Spezialisten zum erfolgreichen Abschluss einer Projektsentwicklung notwendig ist.

Der Einfluss der Form und Sequenzen des Raumes auf die Gestaltung des Image, dank der Mechanik der Rauminhalte, ist so wichtig, wie auch die

All of this implies that, while aesthetics are relevant when shaping these spaces, it is necessary to combine practicality, functionality and order in the space, all of which are key characteristics that help the client to trust, and accept, the product or service offered.

Before anything, it must be understood that under this paradigm, the design is oriented at interpreting the clients' needs and generating new ones using persuasive stimulus; all of this is related both to meeting those needs and the person's well-being and the benefit of the project itself.

As can be seen, it is best to carefully consider the design of these spaces, with talent and imagination being fundamental for keeping in mind functionality, competitiveness and identity.

tengan las superficies; el color de los muros, muebles y accesorios; los criterios en cuanto a la combinación de técnicas y calidades de iluminación; los equipamientos generales y las instalaciones; así como la disposición de todos estos elementos y el modo en el que interactúan entre sí.

Todo ello implica que si bien para modelar estos espacios es relevante tener siempre en cuenta la estética, es imprescindible conjugarla con la practicidad para dotar al sitio de funcionalidad y orden, características indispensables para que el cliente acepte y confíe en el producto o servicio que se le oferta.

Ante todo, hay que entender que en esta tipología el diseño se orienta a interpretar las necesidades de los clientes y a generar en ellos otras nuevas a partir de estímulos persuasivos; todo esto tiene que ver tanto con la satisfacción de dichas necesidades como con el bienestar de la persona y con el beneficio del propio establecimiento.

Come se ve, conviene entonces que el diseño de estos espacios sea operado con una intencionalidad, manteniendo en mente los aspectos de funcionalidad, competitividad e identidad; por lo que dos de los aspectos que será fundamental poner en práctica serán el talento y la imaginación.

la dimension du mobilier qui s'y intègre ; les matériaux et les finitions des surfaces ; la couleur des murs, meubles et accessoires ; les critères appliqués aux mélanges de techniques et qualités d'éclairage ; les équipements généraux et les installations ; ainsi que la disposition de tous ces éléments et la manière dont ils s'influencent entre eux.

S'il est important, pour modeler ces espaces, de toujours prendre en compte l'esthétique, il est indispensable de l' associer à la pratique pour doter le lieu de fonctionnalité et d'ordre, caractéristiques indispensables pour que le client accepte et ait confiance en la qualité du produit ou service qui lui est offert.

Dans ce cas, l'architecture cherche avant tout, à interpréter les besoins des clients et à en générer d'autres en créant des stimulations persuasives ; il faut donc satisfaire leurs besoins et faciliter leur bien être grâce à l'établissement.

Il convient donc que le design de ces espaces soit orienté précisément, maintenant des aspects de fonctionnalité, compétitivité et identité ; c'est pourquoi les aspects fondamentaux à mettre en pratique sont le talent et l'imagination.

verschiedenen Zonen gegeben wird, die Verteilung, Art, Systeme und Maße des dazukommenden Mobiliars; die Materialien und Oberflächenbehandlungen; die Farbe von Wänden, Möbeln und Zubehör; die Kriterien zum Kombinieren von Beleuchtungstechniken und –verteilung; die allgemeine Ausstattung und Installationen; sowohl als auch die Anordnung jedes dieser Elemente und die ihre Interaktionsweise.

Daraus ergibt sich, dass beim Gestalten der Räume die Ästhetik immer im Auge behalten werden muss. Es ist notwendig zum Schaffen von Funktionalität und Ordnung, die unerlässliche Eigenschaften sind, zum Akzeptieren der angebotenen Produkte oder Dienstleistungen durch den Kunden und sein Vertrauen in sie.

Vor allem ist zu verstehen, dass bei dieser Entwurfstypologie man sich nach der Auslegung des Bedürfnisse des Kundens richtet und daran hier durch überzeugende Anreize Neue zu erwecken. All dies hat mit dem Erfüllen solcher Bedürfnisse zu tun, wie auch mit dem Wohlempfinden des Menschen und mit dem Nutzen für das Unternehmen.

Wie man hier sieht, empfiehlt es sich, dass der Entwurf dieser Räume mit Absichtlichkeit geschieht, wobei man Funktionalität, Wettbewerbsfähigkeit und Identität beachtet und die beiden Grundaspekte, Talent und Vorstellungskraft in die Praxis umgesetzt werden.

colour
color
couleur
farbe

Se terminó de imprimir en el mes de Julio del 2005 en Hong Kong. El cuidado de la edición estuvo a cargo de AM Editores S.A. de C.V.

hotels
hoteles
hôtels
hotels

SENSITIVITY TOWARD COLORS is not merely a physical occurrence, it is emotional and psychological as well; therefore, the chromatic choices for a hotel must take into account a series of factors, which include the weather and orientation of the site, the function of each space, the encouragement of particular feelings and activities, as well the intended image and impression.

LA SENSIBILIDAD HACIA LOS COLORES no es sólo un hecho físico sino también emocional y psicológico; por esta razón la selección cromática para un hotel debe realizarse de acuerdo con el estudio de una serie de factores, entre los que destacan el clima y la orientación del sitio, las funciones de cada uno de los espacios, la estimulación hacia determinadas sensaciones y actividades, así como la imagen e impresión que se desee causar.

LA SENSIBILITÉ AUX COULEURS n'est pas seulement physique, c'est aussi une sensation émotionnelle et psychologique ; c'est pourquoi la sélection chromatique d'un hôtel doit être réalisée selon l'étude d'une série de facteurs, parmi lesquels le climat et l'orientation du lieu, les fonctions de chacun des espaces, la stimulation créée par des sensations et activités déterminées, et l'image et l'impression que l'on souhaite donner.

FARBEMPFINDSAMKEIT ist nicht nur eine physiologische Tatsache, sondern auch eine emotionale und psychologische, wodurch die Wahl der Farbpalette für ein Hotel erst nach dem Untersuchen von Faktoren getroffen werden darf, unter denen sich das Klima, die Ausrichtung des Gebäudes, die Funktion jedes Raumes und das Erwecken bestimmter Gefühle und Aktivitäten behaupten, wie auch Gesamtbild und Eindruck, die geschaffen werden sollen.

The choice of color for the spaces of a hotel is related to the promises and expectations generated in the client; if a dynamic and fun stay is promoted, it is best that warm colors predominate in common areas, because they have the ability to stimulate, energize and favor physical and mental activities; when rest is sought, choosing a gamut of cold colors helps to create a relaxed, calm and peaceful atmosphere.

El color que se elija para los espacios de un hotel tiene que ver con las expectativas que se generen en el cliente; si lo que se promueve es una estancia dinámica y divertida será mejor que en áreas comunes dominen los colores cálidos que tienen la capacidad de estimular, energizar y favorecer las actividades físicas y cerebrales; cuando a lo que se invita es al descanso, elegir una gama de colores fríos ayudará a que el ambiente sea de relajación, tranquilidad y serenidad.

Le choix d'une couleur pour les espaces d'un hôtel doit correspondre aux promesses faites au client et à ses expectatives ; si on propose un séjour dynamique et amusant, il faut appliquer des couleurs chaudes qui ont la capacité de stimuler, donner de l'énergie et favoriser les activités physiques et cérébrales ; lorsque l'on invite au repos, il est conseillé de sélectionner une gamme de couleurs froides qui aidera à ce que l'ambiance détende, tranquillise et inspire la sérénité.

Die für Räumlichkeiten in Hotels gewählten Farben beziehen sich auf die beim Gast erweckten Versprechen und Erwartungen. Wurde ein dynamischer und unterhaltsamer Aufenthalt angeboten, dann sollten in den Gemeinschaftsbereichen warme Farben dominieren, die anregen, Energie spenden und körperliche und geistige Aktivitäten fördern.

While the rooms of a hotel need color as an aesthetic tool, it is best that the tones help to maintain balance in the guest's mood. White and the light, soft tones of cold colors reflect calm, convey a feeling of peace, and allow one to rest well; when they are further combined with materials that have natural warm colors, such as wood and brick, immensely comfortable atmospheres are created. These environments are enhanced if they are accompanied by indirect or yellow light.

Si bien las habitaciones de un hotel necesitan del color como una herramienta estética, conviene que los tonos que se usen cooperen a mantener un equilibrio en el estado de ánimo del huésped. El blanco y los matices claros y tenues de los colores fríos reflejan calma, hacen sentir paz y permiten descansar; cuando se combinan con materiales que naturalmente poseen colores cálidos, como la madera o el ladrillo, se generan atmósferas altamente acogedoras. Estos ambientes se enriquecen si se acompañan de una iluminación indirecta con luz amarillenta.

Lorsque la couleur d'une chambre d'hôtel est un outil esthétique, les tons doivent contribuer à maintenir un équilibre pour le client. Le blanc et les nuances claires et discrètes des couleurs froides reflètent la tranquillité, inspirent la paix et permettent de bien se reposer ; lorsqu'elles sont aussi mélangées avec des matériaux qui ont naturellement des couleurs chaudes comme le bois ou la brique, on crée des atmosphères très accueillantes. Ces ambiances s'enrichissent si on les accompagne d'un éclairage indirect avec une lumière jaune.

Wenn Hotelräume die Farbe als ästhetisches Instrument nutzen, empfiehlt es sich, dass die verwendeten Tön mithelfen den Gemütszustand des Gastes im Gleichgewicht zu halten. Weiß und helle, sanfte Schattierungen der kalten Farben bringen Ruhe, erwecken das Gefühl des Friedens und lassen richtig Ausruhen. Wenn sie dazu mit Materialien kombiniert werden, die von Natur her warme Farben besitzen, wie Holz und Ziegelstein, dann werden höchst gemütliche Atmosphären geschaffen. Die Gegenwart von indirekter Beleuchtung durch gelbes Licht verstärkt diese Ambiente noch.

The mixture of yellow, ochre and orange with different degrees of saturation on the furniture, surfaces, coatings and in the lighting creates cheerful, warm and vital atmospheres, because they are stimulating colors.

La mezcla de amarillos, ocres y naranjas en distintos grados de saturación, tanto en mobiliario como en superficies, recubrimientos e iluminación, crea ambientes alegres, cálidos y vitales, pues todos éstos son colores estimulantes.

Le mélange de couleurs stimulantes telles que le jaune, ocre ou orange de différentes intensités, dans le mobilier, les murs, les recouvrements et l'éclairage crée des ambiances joyeuses, chaleureuses et vitales.

Mischungen von Gelb, Ocker und Orange zu verschiedenen Sättigungsgraden, sowohl im Mobiliar, wie auch in Oberflächen, Belägen und Beleuchtung schöpfen fröhliche, gemütliche und lebendige Ambiente, da sie anregende Farben sind.

MIS SUEÑOS FLUYEN A TRAVÉS DE LA LENTE Y SE CRISTALIZAN EN TUS PUPILAS...

In tropical weather, it is important to incorporate colors into the furniture and building materials that come from natural fibers, such as stems, palm leaves, adobe and brick; these tones go very well with walls or floors with earth tones and with upholstery or bed linen in raw and white colors.

En climas tropicales es importante integrar a la composición cromática los colores de las fibras naturales de los muebles y de los materiales de construcción como troncos, hojas de palma, adobes y ladrillos; estos tonos van muy bien con los muros y pisos con tendencia a las gamas térreas, así como con las tapicerías y ropa de cama en colores crudos y blancos.

Dans les climats tropicaux, il est important d'intégrer
à la composition chromatique les couleurs des fibres
naturelles des meubles et matériaux comme les troncs,
feuilles de palme, pisés et briques ; ces tons s'assortissent
très bien avec des murs ou sols de couleur terre et
avec les tissus d'ameublement ou linge de maison de
couleurs crues et blanches.

Im Tropenklima ist es wichtig, die Farben der Naturfasern
der Möbel und Baumaterialien, wie Baumstämme,
Palmenblätter, Lehmziegel und Backsteine in die
Farbenkomposition zu integrieren. Ihre Farbtöne
kombinieren sehr gut mit den erdfarbigen Tendenzen
der Wände und Fußböden und mit Dekorstoffen und
Bettwäsche aus rohen oder weißen Farben.

It must be noted that color and paint are two different things and that building materials have a natural color. When buildings are inserted into natural landscapes, it is best that their exteriors be related to the environment; one way to achieve this is by integrating building materials supplied by the land itself, because they have a color that harmonizes with the habitat. Continuing the idea of relating to the site, if any paint is used on the walls, it is preferable to use warm colors -ochre, yellow and terra cotta-.

Hay que tener en cuenta que color y pintura son dos cosas distintas y que los materiales de construcción poseen un color natural. Cuando las construcciones se insertan en paisajes naturales conviene que sus exteriores se relacionen con el entorno; una forma de lograrlo es integrar los materiales constructivos que ofrece la propia tierra, pues éstos poseen un color que está en armonía con el hábitat. Para seguir con la idea de pertenencia al lugar, si se utiliza pintura en los muros, es preferible usar colores cálidos -ocres, amarillos y terracotas-.

Il faut prendre en compte que couleur et peinture sont deux choses différentes et que les matériaux ont une couleur naturelle. Lorsque les constructions s'insèrent dans des paysages naturels, leurs extérieurs doivent se mettre en relation avec leur entourage. Pour y parvenir, on peut intégrer des matériaux naturels, ayant des couleurs en harmonie avec l'habitat. Pour continuer avec l'idée d'appartenance au lieu, si l'on utilise de la peinture sur les murs, il faudra utiliser des couleurs chaudes –ocres, jaunes et terra cotas–.

Es ist wichtig zu bedenken, dass Farbe und Anstrich nicht das Gleiche sind und dass Baustoffe ihre eigene natürliche Farbe besitzen. Um Gebäude in natürliche Landschaften einzufügen, sollten ihre Außenräume in Beziehung zur Umgebung stehen. Eine Methode, um das zu erreichen, ist das Integrieren von Baustoffen, die die Natur selbst anbietet, da deren Farbe harmonisch in den natürlichen Lebensraum passt. Beim Weiterverfolgen der Idee des Hingehörens, sollte man für Wandanstriche warmen Tönen, wie Ocker, Gelb und Terrakotta den Vorzug geben.

The proportion between scale, color and volume is a determining factor in the design of a hotel. The color of its exteriors requires aesthetic sensitivity for establishing a balance between the size and the substance of its bodies and the colors in the landscape; the use of colors that are similar and mimic those of the environs contributes to the overall harmony.

La proporción entre escala, color y volumen es determinante en el diseño de un hotel. El color de sus exteriores requiere de sensibilidad estética para establecer un equilibrio entre las dimensiones y solidez de sus cuerpos y la tonalidad existente en el paisaje; el uso de colores que se parezcan a los dominantes en el entorno y se mimeticen con él, cooperan a la armonía.

La proportion entre l'échelle, la couleur et le volume est déterminante pour un hôtel. La sensibilité esthétique dédiée au choix de la couleur des extérieurs aide à établir un équilibre entre les dimensions, la solidité de leurs corps et les tonalités du paysage ; l'emploi de couleurs ressemblant aux dominantes de l'environnement et qui les imite, contribue à l'harmonie.

Das Verhältnis zwischen Maßstab, Farbe und Rauminhalt ist entscheidend für das Hoteldesign. Die Farbe der Außenräume verlangt ästhetische Empfindsamkeit für das Gleichgewicht zwischen Maßen und Festigkeit ihrer Körper und den Farbtönen der Landschaft. Die Verwendung von Farben, die denen, die die Umgebung dominieren ähnlich sind und dadurch in ihr untertauchen, stärken die Harmonie.

A monochromatic composition using tones from the same palette on the floors, walls, furniture and lighting enhances the image of a space as a whole; but it is also beneficial to include plants and details in neutral colors that break the monotony.

Una composición monocromática usando tonos de la misma gama en los pisos, muros, mobiliario e iluminación, refuerza la imagen unitaria de un espacio; pero beneficia incluir plantas o detalles en colores neutros que rompan la monotonía.

Une composition monochromatique de tons d'une même gamme sur les sols, murs, mobilier et éclairage renforce l'image d'un espace ; mais il est utile d'inclure des plantes ou des détails de couleurs neutres qui rompent la monotonie.

Eine einfarbige Komposition, die die gleiche Farbpalette in Fußböden, Wänden, Mobiliar und Beleuchtung benutzt, stärkt das Einheitsbild des Raumes, wobei das Beifügen von Pflanzen oder Details in Neutraltönen die Monotonie bricht.

In the construction, it is best to use colors that imitate the surrounding environment, so that nature's own color defines the atmosphere.

Para que sea el propio color de la naturaleza circundante el que defina un ambiente, es necesario que en la arquitectura se usen colores que la imiten.

Afin que la couleur de la nature environnante définisse une ambiance, il est nécessaire d'employer dans l'architecture des couleurs qui l'imitent.

Damit die Farbe, die der umgebenden Natur eigen ist, ein Ambiente bestimmt, müssen bei der Architektur Töne benutzt werden, die sie nachahmen.

offices oficinas bureaux büroräume

Color in the most influential design tool in the image of a commercial or utility building; its selection must be thoroughly considered.

El color es la herramienta de diseño que mayor fuerza tiene en la imagen de cualquier edificio comercial o de servicios; por lo que su selección debe ser muy cuidada.

La couleur est l'outil de design qui a le plus de force dans l'image d'une construction commerciale ou de services ; son choix doit donc être très soigné.

Als Designinstrument bei Geschäfts- oder Dienstleistungsbauten übt Farbe den stärksten Einfluss auf das Gesamtbild aus, weshalb sie sehr vorsichtig gewählt werden muss.

LIGHTING is an essential factor for the office work process. To a large degree, the radiance of a space is related to the amount of light or dark colors it has; to achieve a well-lit ambience, the use of light tones must be favored, if they are applied on sleek surfaces, light will be better reflected.

LA ILUMINACIÓN es un factor esencial para el desarrollo del trabajo en oficinas. En buena medida, la luminosidad de un espacio se relaciona con la cantidad de colores claros u oscuros que contiene; para lograr un ambiente con luz se debe favorecer el predominio de tonos claros que, si además se aplican sobre superficies lisas, éstas ayudarán a reflejar la luz.

DANS LES BUREAUX, l'éclairage est un facteur de travail essentiel, et la luminosité d'un espace a une relation directe avec la quantité de couleurs claires ou obscures dont il est décoré ; pour obtenir une ambiance lumineuse, il faut favoriser les tons clairs qui, s'ils sont appliqués sur des surfaces lisses, aideront à refléter la lumière.

DIE BELEUCHTUNG ist ein wesentlicher Faktor für dem Arbeitsablauf im Büroraum. Die Menge heller und dunkler Farben, die er enthält, ist ausschlaggebend für die Leuchtkraft des Raumes. Um ein Ambiente voller Licht zu schaffen, müssen helle Töne vorherrschen. Wenn sie dazu noch auf glatte Oberflächen aufgetragen werden, so wird das Licht von diesen widergespiegelt.

In a color composition that seeks elegance, it is preferable to limit the color range.

En una composición de color en la que lo que se busca es elegancia, es preferible que la elección sea restringida.

Pour obtenir une élégante composition de couleurs, il est préférable d'en restreindre le nombre.

In einer Farbkomposition bei der Eleganz gesucht wird, ist es zu empfehlen eine begrenzte Wahl vorzuziehen.

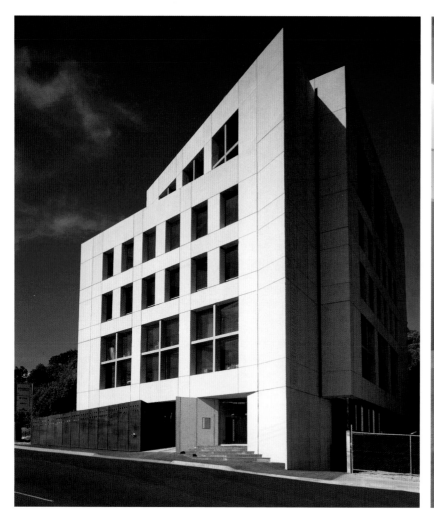

The shape, color, light and texture of the architectural and decorative elements convey their own expressive characteristics. Shapes contain colors and textures, but these only have meaning in the presence of light; therefore, when molding and designing the space, it is necessary to think of the choices of mixing these factors holistically, in order to achieve balanced volumes, with harmonic visual weight and rhythm. Taking into account the finishes of the materials is especially relevant for achieving this goal.

La forma, el color, la luz y la textura de los elementos arquitectónicos y decorativos transmiten características de expresión propias. La forma contiene al color y a las texturas, pero éstos sólo cobran sentido en presencia de la luz; de manera que para modelar y diseñar el espacio hay que pensar en las opciones de combinar la totalidad de estos factores para lograr volúmenes en equilibrio y con un peso y ritmo visual armónico. Tomar en cuenta los acabados de los materiales tiene especial relevancia para alcanzar este objetivo.

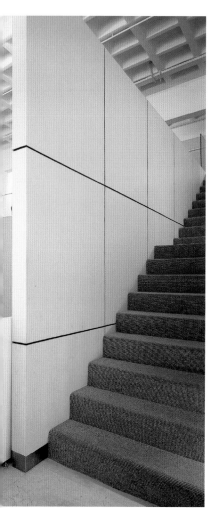

La forme, la couleur, la lumière et la texture des éléments architecturaux et décoratifs transmettent des caractéristiques d'expression propres. La forme englobe couleur et textures, et prend tout son sens en présence de la lumière ; de sorte que pour modeler et dessiner l'espace, il faut penser aux possibilités de mélanger la totalité de ces facteurs pour obtenir des volumes équilibrés avec un poids et un rythme visuel harmonieux. Pour atteindre cet objectif, il est important de prendre en compte les finitions des matériaux.

Form, Farbe, Licht und Textur der architektonischen und dekorativen Elemente vermitteln ihre eigenen Ausdrucksweisen. Die Form enthält die Farbe und die Texturen, die allerdings nur in Gegenwart von Licht einen Sinn bekommen. Deshalb muss beim Gestalten und Entwerfen des Raumes an die möglichen Kombinationen der Töne dieser Faktoren gedacht werden, um ausgewogene Rauminhalte zu schaffen mit harmonischem visuellen Gewicht und Rhythmus, was durch das Beachten der Relevanz der Oberflächen der Materialien erreicht wird.

Of all colors, white is the most radiant and the one most commonly associated with feelings of size, cleanliness and coolness; it can blend with virtually every building material and it maintains its properties when mixed with transparencies. Using it as the sole color may come across as sophisticated; however, care must be used when using it in faintly lit places, as it acquires a grayish aspect; on the other hand, its radiance is favored when confronted to natural and artificial halogen light with mauve shades.

De todos los colores el blanco es el de más luminosidad y al que mayormente se le asocia con sensaciones de amplitud, limpieza y frescura; es capaz de armonizar con prácticamente todos los materiales de construcción y combinado con transparencias mantiene estas propiedades. Utilizarlo como única tonalidad puede resultar sofisticado; sin embargo, hay que tener cuidado al recurrir a él en lugares con poca luz, pues obtiene un aspecto grisáceo; por el contrario, frente a la luz natural y a la artificial halógena que tiene tonalidad malva se favorece su resplandor.

De toutes les couleurs, le blanc est la plus lumineuse et celle à laquelle on associe le plus souvent des sensations d'amplitude, pureté et fraîcheur ; elle est capable de se mettre en harmonie avec pratiquement tous les matériaux de construction et elle maintient ces propriétés, ajoutée à des transparences. L'utiliser comme unique tonalité peut résulter sophistiqué. Il faut cependant prendre soin d'avoir recours à des lieux peu illuminés, où l'on obtient un aspect gris ; ou face à la lumière naturelle ou halogène qui lui donne une tonalité mauve et resplendissante.

Weiß besitzt von allen Farbtönen die größte Leuchtkraft und erweckt auch am meisten Gefühle von Großräumigkeit, Sauberkeit und Frische. Es steht eigentlich mit allen Baustoffen im Einklang und beim Kombinieren mit transparenten Materialien behält es seine Eigenschaften. Es als einzigen Ton zu benutzen, wirkt anspruchsvoll, doch ist Vorsicht geboten, wenn Weiß an Stellen mit wenig Licht verwendet wird, da es dort grau aussieht. In der Gegenwart von natürlichem Licht und bei künstlichem malvenfarbenen Halogenlicht, strahlt es dagegen.

Different colors of wood give the impression of being in warm atmospheres, and they can be combined with an extensive gamut of color choices.

Los distintos colores de la madera provocan la impresión de estar en atmósferas cálidas y se les puede combinar con una extensa gama de opciones cromáticas.

Les différentes tonalités du bois donnent à l'atmosphère des tonalités chaleureuses qui peuvent s'assortir à une ample gamme de couleurs.

Durch die unterschiedlichen Holzfarben fühlt man sich in gemütlichen Atmosphären und man kann sie mit einer vielfältigen Farbpalette kombinieren.

Using black and white with metal materials such as stainless steel or aluminum within well-lit spaces with furniture with simple lines creates a modern impression.

La asociación del negro y el blanco con materiales metálicos como el acero inoxidable o el aluminio, en contextos muy iluminados y mobiliario con líneas simples, invita a pensar en ambientes modernos.

L'association de noir, blanc et de matériaux métalliques comme l'acier inoxydable ou l'aluminium, dans des contextes illuminés et un mobilier de lignes simples invite à penser à des ambiances modernes.

Das Zusammenwirken von Schwarz und Weiß mit metallen Materialien, wie Edelstahl oder Aluminium, in stark beleuchteten Umgebungen und bei Mobiliar mit einfachen Linien, lässt an moderne Ambiente denken.

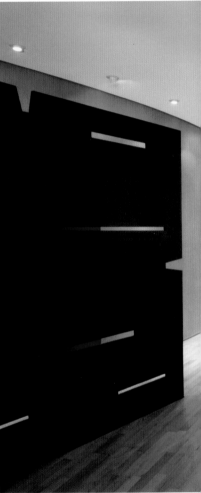

Wood and glass are definitely the materials that best allow for perceiving the temperature of the color; the former evokes warmth while the latter reminds us of ice. When wood is used to cover the larger surfaces and a space is enclosed with glass walls, it creates the feeling of being in front of a floating and transparent space. Lighting has a major role in causing this effect; whether natural or artificial, the light should be focused.

Seguramente son la madera y el vidrio los materiales que mejor permiten percibir la temperatura del color; la primera evoca calidez en tanto que el segundo recuerda al hielo. Cuando se utiliza la madera para cubrir las superficies de mayores dimensiones y se encierra algún espacio entre muros acristalados se provocará la impresión de estar frente a un volumen flotante y transparente. En este efecto tiene un papel primordial la iluminación, la cual, ya sea natural o artificial, se debe procurar que sea puntual.

Des matériaux comme le bois et le verre permettent définitivement de percevoir la température d'une couleur ; le premier évoque la chaleur et le second rappelle la glace. En utilisant le bois pour couvrir les surfaces de grandes dimensions et en enfermant un espace entre des murs de verre, on crée l'impression d'être en face d'un volume flottant et transparent. Avec cet effet, l'éclairage a un rôle primordial, lequel, naturel ou artificiel, doit être ponctuel.

Holz und Glas sind die Materialien, die am besten die Temperatur der Farbe empfinden lassen, Holz das Gefühl von Wärme und Glas, das erinnert an Eis. Wenn Holz zum Bedecken größerer Flächen benutzt und ein Raum zwischen verglasten Wänden damit eingefasst wird, gibt es den Eindruck von einem schwebenden, transparenten Rauminhalt. Hierzu spielt sowohl die natürliche, wie auch die künstliche Beleuchtung eine grundlegende Rolle. Allerdings sollte sie auf Punkte konzentriert sein.

Today, when the trend is to create open office spaces where people can interact, exploring different combinations of color and transparent materials is a flexible and expressive design resource. Glass is useful for delimiting spaces and its degree of opacity defines their visual continuity; sometimes it is its own cold color that sets the tone in the general ambiance, and at other times it is the chromatic composition, whether warm or cold, of floors, walls and ceilings that creates this perception.

Hoy que la tendencia es a crear espacios de oficina abiertos en los que la gente pueda interactuar, explorar las combinaciones entre el color y los materiales transparentes puede resultar un recurso de diseño de gran plasticidad y expresión. El vidrio sirve para delimitar los espacios y su grado de opacidad define la continuidad visual de los mismos; algunas veces es su propio color frío el que da tonalidad al ambiente general y otras es la composición cromática, cálida o fría, de los pisos, muros y techos la que influye en esta percepción.

Aujourd'hui, la tendance est à créer des bureaux ouverts dans lesquels on favorise les échanges, et les combinaisons de couleurs et de matériaux transparents peuvent y contribuer de façon esthétique et expressive. Le verre délimite les espaces et on peut définir la continuité visuelle voulue grâce à son degré d'opacité ; parfois sa couleur froide donne une tonalité à l'ambiance générale et dans d'autres cas, c'est la composition chromatique, chaude ou froide, des sols, murs et toits qui influence cette perception.

Heute neigt sich die Tendenz zum Schöpfen von offenen Büroraümen für die menschliche Interaktion. Kombinationen von Farbe und transparenten Materialien auszuprobieren, kann zu einem sehr plastischen und ausdrucksvollen Entwurfsmittel werden. Glas dient zum Begrenzen von Räumen und seine Lichtdichte definiert die visuelle Kontinuität derselben. Manchmal ist es die kalte Glasfarbe, die den Ton des Ambiente bestimmt und andere Male die Farbkomposition, warm oder kalt, der Böden, Wände und Decken, die diese Sinneswahrnehmung beeinflussen.

Walls and furniture in colors found in nature, especially those related to earth, such as ochre, red, yellow, amber and terra cotta, combined with the greens in the flower boxes or flower pots, give the common areas of an office a mellow and warm feeling, producing comfortable atmospheres. Playing with shapes and varying textures, creating contrast between light and shadow, as well as hanging objects at different heights, allows for emphasizing the qualities of chromatic regularity while at the same time breaking its potential monotony.

Los muros y muebles con colores que se encuentran en la naturaleza, especialmente los relacionados con la tierra como el ocre, rojo, amarillo, ámbar y terracota, aunados a los verdes de las plantas en jardineras o macetas, dotan a los espacios de oficinas de uso comunitario de una sensación de suavidad y calidez, componiendo atmósferas acogedoras. Jugar con las formas, variar las texturas, crear contrastes de luz y sombra, así como colocar objetos en distintas alturas, permitirá exaltar las cualidades de la regularidad cromática y al mismo tiempo quebrantar su posible monotonía.

Les murs et meubles de couleurs naturelles, et notamment celles qui ont une relation avec la terre comme l'ocre, le rouge, le jaune, l'ambre et le terra cota, ajoutés aux verts des plantes en jardinières ou en pots, dotent les bureaux à usage collectif d'une sensation de douceur et de chaleur, créant une atmosphère accueillante. Jouer avec les formes, varier les textures, créer des contrastes de lumière et d'ombre, et agencer des objets à différentes hauteurs, amplifie les qualités de la régularité chromatique et évite la monotonie.

Wände und Möbel mit Farben, die aus der Natur stammen, vor allem die Erdfaben, wie Ocker, Rot, Gelb, Amber und Terrakota, zusammen mit dem Grün der Pflanzen der Blumenkästen oder –töpfe, schenken den Gemeinschaftsräumen der Büros ein Gefühl von Sanftheit und Wärme, wodurch einladende Ambiente geschaffen werden. Mit den Formen zu spielen, die Texturen zu variieren, Kontraste von Licht und Schatten zu schöpfen, sowie das Aufstellen von Objekten auf verschiedene Höhen, ermöglicht das Hervorheben der Eigenschaften der Farbregelmäßigkeit und zugleich das Brechen der Monotonie.

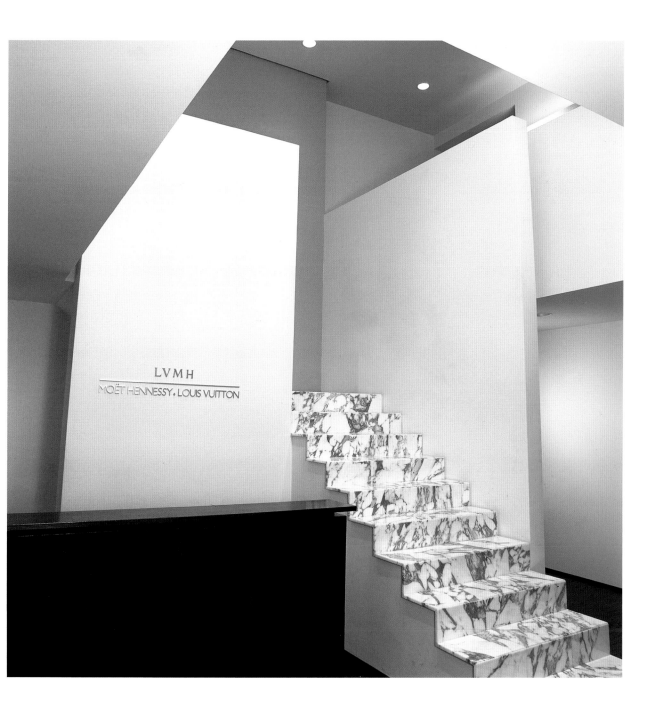

Including the bare minimum in a space, with few objects and sober lines, means limited color content and few tones that are as neutral as possible.

Incluir en un espacio sólo lo necesario, pocas cosas y de líneas muy sobrias, puede sugerir también contenidos de color limitados, un mínimo de tonalidades tan neutras como sea posible.

Inclure dans un espace le strict nécessaire, c'est-à-dire peu d'objets de lignes sobres, avec un nombre de couleurs limité, un minimum de tonalités, les plus neutres possibles.

In einen Raum nur das Nötigste, durch wenige Dinge mit nüchteren Linien, einzuführen, empfiehlt dann auch Inhalte von begrenzter Farbe, mit so wenigen und so neutralen Tönen wie möglich.

A color composition alternative that may turn out to be attractive is using two colors, degrading them to produce several tones and making both equally relevant in the whole scheme. This two-color chromatic communion will require a third color to discreetly burst into the scheme, which can be introduced using a piece of furniture or an accessory, although light is always the best intruder.

Una alternativa compositiva de color que puede resultar muy atrayente, es recurrir a dos colores degradándolos para conformar distintos matices y hacer que ambos tengan igual peso en todo el esquema. Esta comunión dicromática necesitará de un tercer color que irrumpa de forma discreta y que puede ser introducido en un mueble o un accesorio, aunque el mejor intruso siempre será la luz.

La conjugaison de deux couleurs notamment en les dégradant pour former des nuances et leur donner le même poids dans toute la décoration donne un résultat splendide. Cette communion de couleurs devra être discrètement interrompue par une troisième couleur, qui pourra être introduite sur un meuble ou un accessoire, cependant, l'intrus le plus intéressant reste la lumière.

Eine attraktive Alternative der Farbkomposition ist das Verwenden von zwei Farben, mit denen man durch Abtönen Schattierungen schafft, dabei müssen beide im ganzen Schema das gleiche Gewicht haben. Diese zweifarbige Gemeinschaft braucht noch eine dritte Farbe, die diskret unterbricht und in einem Möbelstück oder Zubehör eingeführt wird. Trotzdem ist der beste Eindringling immer das Licht.

If brown, ochre and sand shades are used on furniture, floors, ceilings and walls, and the light is also based on a warm palette, it is possible to create cozy, elegant and visually sharp spaces; that perception has further consequences when it is combined with the ideas of sparse furnishings and simple, pure lines. Small openings, moldings, rugged surfaces, reliefs, bas-reliefs, and superimposed spaces are among the elements that can be explored on furniture and walls, and facilitate the creation of shadow effects.

Si se utilizan gamas que desciendan del café, del ocre y del arena, tanto en los muebles como en los pisos, techos y paredes, y la iluminación se basa también en una coloración cálida, es posible crear ambientes acogedores, elegantes y de impresión visual nítida; esta última percepción tiene mayores consecuencias cuando se fusiona con la idea de pocos muebles y de líneas simples y puras. Pequeños vanos, molduras, estriados, realces, bajorrelieves, superposición de volúmenes, entre otros elementos con los que se puede jugar tanto en el mobiliario como en los muros, permitirán crear efectos de sombra.

Les gammes provenant du marron, de l'ocre et du sable pour les meubles comme les sols, plafonds et murs, et un éclairage basé sur un ton chaud, ajouté à un mobilier de lignes simples et pures, créent des ambiances accueillantes, élégantes et limpides. D'autres éléments avec lesquels on peut jouer dans le mobilier et les murs, sont les petites ouvertures, les moulures, les rayures, les reliefs et bas-reliefs, la superposition de volumes, entre autres, pour créer des effets d'ombre.

Wenn für Möbel, Böden, Decken und Wände von Braun, Ocker und Sandfarben abstammende Farbpaletten benutzt werden und die Beleuchtung auch warme Farben zeigt, dann ist es möglich, einladende, elegante Ambiente von klarem visuellem Eindruck zu schaffen. Diese Wahrnehmung hat wichtigere Folgen, wenn sie mit wenigen Möbeln mit einfachen und reinen Linien kombiniert wird. Kleine Öffnungen, Zierleisten, Rillen, Hoch- und Flachrelief, Überlagerung von Rauminhalten und andere Elemente mit denen man am Mobiliar und an den Wänden spielen kann, ermöglichen das Schaffen von Schatteneffekten.

It is true that building materials have characteristics of their own that make them unmistakable, among them, texture, consistency and natural color; to name just a few, concrete is a rubbery gray, glass is transparent, and brick has a reddish color. However, the appearance of the color of these materials can be modified, if so desired. One possibility for very pleasant visual effects is exposing the material in combination, that is, showing its natural color in a fragmented way.

Es cierto que los materiales de construcción tienen características propias que los hacen inconfundibles, entre ellas está su textura, consistencia y su coloración natural; el concreto posee un color gris chicle, el vidrio es transparente, la tonalidad del ladrillo es rojiza, por sólo nombrar algunos. Sin embargo, y si así se desea, a estos materiales se les puede modificar su apariencia y color natural. Una posibilidad que tiene efectos visuales muy agradables es la exposición del material de forma combinada, es decir, interviniendo en su color natural solamente de forma fragmentada.

Il est certain que les matériaux de construction ont des caractéristiques propres qui les rendent uniques, telles que leur texture, consistance et coloration naturelle, pour n'en nommer que quelques uns, le ciment a une couleur grise, le verre est transparent, la brique a des tonalités rouges. Cependant, si on le souhaite, on peut modifier la couleur apparente de ces matériaux. Pour créer des effets visuels très agréables, on peut exposer des matériaux mélangés, c'est à dire, qui interviennent dans leur couleur naturelle de manière fragmentée.

Es stimmt, dass Baustoffe charakteristische Eigenschaften haben, die sie unverwechselbar machen, darunter befindet sich die Textur, die Stoffbeschaffenheit und die natürliche Färbung. Der Beton hat eine Farbe wie grauer Gummi, Glas ist transparent, Ziegelsteine sind rötlich, um nur einige zu nennen. Allerdings kann das farbliche Aussehen dieser Materialien auf Wunsch geändert werden. Eine Möglichkeit, die sehr angenehme visuelle Effekte bietet, ist das kombinierte Vorzeigen es Materials, dass heißt in seine natürliche Farbe bruckstückhaft einzugreifen.

rehab centers
centros de rehabilitación
centres de réhabilitation
zentren der rehabilitation

84

varied spaces
espacios diversos
espaces divers
allerlei räume

ASIDE from the fact that chromotherapy, or using color to treat disease, is evolving, today it is known that the vibration of colors on the human body has emotional and psychological effects that may help people to relax, or boost their energy. Spaces intended for the physical rehabilitation of children require an icy blend of colors that arouses energy; red, yellow and oranges fit this purpose.

INDEPENDIENTEMENTE de que la cromoterapia o terapia a través de los colores para combatir enfermedades está en evolución, hoy se sabe que la vibración de los colores en el cuerpo humano tiene efectos emocionales y psicológicos que pueden ayudar a una persona a calmarse o a aumentar su energía. Los espacios destinados a la rehabilitación física de niños requieren de una mezcla de colores álgida que despierte la energía; los rojos, amarillos y naranjas son propicios para estos fines.

INDÉPENDAMMENT du fait que la chromothérapie ou thérapie des couleurs est en évolution, il est aujourd'hui reconnu que la vibration des couleurs dans le corps humain a des effets émotionnels et psychologiques qui peuvent aider une personne à se calmer ou à augmenter son énergie. Les espaces destinés à la réhabilitation physique d'enfants requièrent d'un mélange de couleurs chaleureuses qui donnent de l'énergie ; les rouges, jaunes et orange sont indiqués à ces fins.

UNABHÄNGIG davor, dass die Chromotherapie oder Therapie durch Farben zum Bekämpfen von Krankheiten noch in der Entwicklung steckt, weiß man heute schon, dass die Schwingungen der Farben im menschlichen Körper emotionale und psychologische Folgen haben, die helfen den Menschen zu beruhigen oder sein Energieniveau anzuheben. Räume, die der körperlichen Rehabilitierung von Kindern dienen, brauchen eine kraftspendende Farbmischung. Rot-, Gelb- und Orangetöne sind dazu bestens geeignet.

TEXTURES, COLOR AND LIGHT allow the three-dimensional characteristics of space to be admired and are its main components. In buildings with large dimensions, where there is a preponderance of walls over the openings, color gains even more importance, so it is recommended that chromatic compositions are chosen based on a holistic vision, taking into consideration the environment that surrounds the architectural work.

LAS TEXTURAS, EL COLOR Y LA LUZ permiten valorar las características tridimensionales del espacio y se constituyen en sus componentes primordiales. En construcciones de volúmenes masivos, en las que dominan los muros sobre los vanos, el color alcanza mayor relevancia, por lo que es recomendable que la composición cromática que se elija tenga base en la visión de conjunto, considerando también el contexto circundante de la obra arquitectónica.

LES TEXTURES, LA COULEUR ET LA LUMIÈRE permettent d'évaluer les caractéristiques tridimensionnelles de l'espace et en sont des composants essentiels. Dans des constructions massives, où les murs dominent les ouvertures, la couleur atteint une plus grande importance, et il est donc recommandé de choisir une composition chromatique avec une base pour la vision d'ensemble, considérant aussi le contexte environnant de l'oeuvre architecturale.

DIE TEXTUREN, DIE FARBE UND DAS LICHT ermöglichen es, die dreidimensionalen Eigenschaften des Raumes zu erfassen und werden zu dessen elementaren Bestandteilen. In Bauwerken mit massiven Rauminhalten, wo die festen Wände gegenüber der Öffnungen vorherrschen, gewinnt die Farbe an Relevanz, weshalb es ratsam ist, dass die gewählte Farbkomposition sich auf das Gesamtbild bezieht, wobei auch die Umgebung des architektonischen Werkes beachtet wird.

It is possible to play with light, color and shape, even on flat surfaces such as walls and floors, although this is more interesting in three-dimensional spaces, because depth is involved. The strength of colors in every dimension is perceived with a greater impact.

Es posible jugar con la luz, el color y la forma aún en superficies planas como es el caso de muros y pisos, aunque hay que admitir que dicho juego adquiere mayor interés en el espacio tridimensional, pues se le agrega la dimensión de la profundidad y la fuerza de los colores en todas las dimensiones se percibe con mayor impacto.

Il est possible de jouer avec la lumière, la couleur et la forme même sur des surfaces planes comme les murs et les sols, bien qu'il faille admettre que ce jeu prend un plus grand intérêt dans l'espace, qui ajoute de la profondeur. La force des couleurs dans toutes les dimensions a un impact majeur.

Sogar bei ebenen Flächen kann man mit Licht, Farbe und Form spielen, wie etwas bei Wänden und Böden. Allerdings muss erwähnt werden, dass dieses Spiel eine größere Beachtung des dreidimensionalen Raumes verlangt, da die Dimension, Tiefe, dazu kommt, wodurch die Kraft der Farben in allen Dimensionen stärker wahrnehmbar wird.

The ceilings in rehab centers are high; if color is applied, it is best that there is only one, and that attention is centered on light.

Los techos de los centros de rehabilitación son extensos; si se les aplica color conviene que sea uno solo y que se centre la atención en la luz.

Les plafonds des centres de réhabilitation étant étendus ; il convient de n'appliquer qu'une seule couleur et de prendre soin de l'éclairage.

In Zentren der Rehabilitation sind Decken weitläufig. Sie sollten einfarbig angestrichen werden und die Aufmerksamkeit aufs Licht lenken.

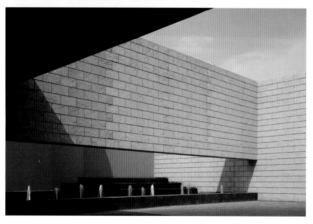

clubhouse   casa club   foyer du club   clubhaus

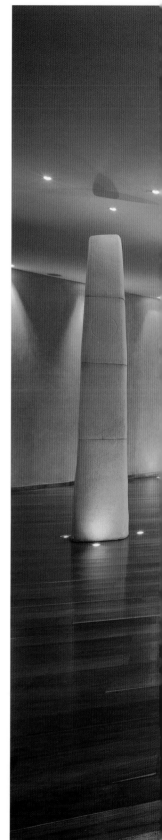

When the background color is more saturated and stronger than colors in the foreground planes, it becomes the predominant color and influences the way other colors are perceived. A hierarchy of planes and volumes may be created if special attention is given to this fact, because strong and noticeable colors will give a space an extroverted personality, while soft ones, when contrasted with the former, diminish their own expression within the building.

Cuando el color del fondo de una edificación es más saturado y tiene más fuerza que los que se observan en los primeros planos, se constituirá en el tono dominante e influirá en la manera en que se perciban todos los colores que se le superpongan. Se puede crear una jerarquía de planos y volúmenes si se pone atención en este hecho, ya que los colores fuertes y llamativos le podrán dar carácter extrovertido a un cuerpo, mientras que los suaves, cuando se encuentren frente a aquéllos, menguarán su expresión dentro de la construcción.

Lorsque la couleur du fond est plus saturée et a plus de force que celles qui s'observent dans les premiers plans, on en fera le ton dominant qui influencera la perception de toutes les couleurs qui s'y superposent. On peut créer une hiérarchie de plans et volumes si on y fait attention, puisque les couleurs fortes et voyantes pourront donner un caractère extraverti à un corps, alors que les douces, qui y sont juxtaposées, auront une expression réduite dans l'ensemble.

Wenn die Farbe des Hintergrunds gesättigter und kräftiger ist, als die im Vordergrund zu betrachtenden Farben, wird sie zum dominierenden Ton und beeinflusst die Weise, auf die alle Farben, die sie begleiten, wahrgenommen werden. Man kann eine Rangordnung von Ebenen und Rauminhalten schaffen, wenn man diese Tatsache beachtet, da die kräftigen Farben mit ihrem Hervorstehen dem Körper einen extrovertierten Charakter geben können, während die sanften Töne, durch ihre Gegenwart, dessen Ausdruckskraft im Bauwerk schmälern.

Contrasts between colors used on the façades of architectural works help to create different perceptions of the space, for example, closeness and distance, among others, and through these, there is a play between the different architectural levels. Likewise, the color of the landscape plays a major role, given that, aside from being intense and vital, it generates shadows on parts of the walls throughout the day, giving their colors a different palette.

Los contrastes de los colores en las fachadas de las obras arquitectónicas cooperan a crear distintas percepciones del espacio, entre ellas las de cercanía y lejanía, a través de las cuales se concibe una dinámica entre los diversos planos arquitectónicos. Asimismo, adquiere un lugar preponderante del paisaje, ya que además de ser intenso y vital, genera a lo largo de las distintas horas del día algunas sombras sobre determinadas porciones de los muros que le dan otra tonalidad al color de los mismos.

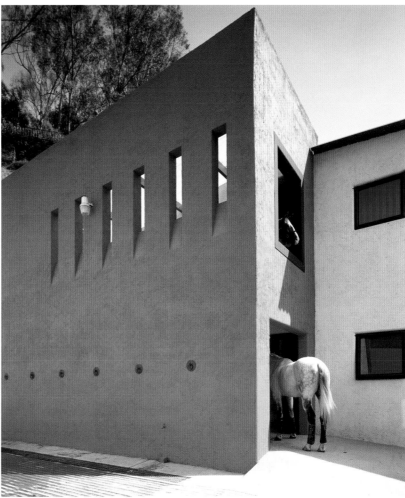

es contrastes entre les couleurs des façades des oeuvres architecturales contribuent à créer différentes perceptions de l'espace, comme la proximité et l'éloignement, à travers lesquelles on conçoit une dynamique entre les divers plans architecturaux. De même, la couleur du paysage est primordiale, intense et vitale, elle génère des ombres sur des portions de murs en leur donnant des tonalités changeantes tout au long de la journée.

Die Kontraste, die zwischen den Farben der Fassaden der architektonischen Werke entstehen, unterstützen die Schöpfung erschiedener Wahrnehmungen des Raumes, darunter die von Nah und Fern, wodurch eine Dynamik zwischen den unterschiedlichen architektonischen Ebenen empfindbar wird. So gewinnt auch die Farbe der Landschaft eine ausschlaggebende Stellung, da sie außer intensiv und lebendig, auch noch zu verschiedenen Tageszeiten Schatten auf estimmten Wandabschnitten schafft, die der Farbe derselben andere Töne schenken.

To enhance the unified character of the space, sometimes it is best to use similar colors on the floors, pillars and low walls that make up the open spaces of clubs.

Para reforzar el carácter de unidad y de conjunto de la arquitectura algunas veces conviene usar colores similares en los pisos, pilares y muretes que conforman sus espacios abiertos.

Pour renforcer le caractère homogène d'un espace, il convient quelques fois d'utiliser des couleurs similaires sur les sols, piliers, murets des espaces ouverts des clubs.

Um Eigenschaften von Einheit oder Zusammengehören der Räume zu verstärken, empfiehlt es sich, für Böden, Pfeiler und Niedrigwände der offenen Räume der Clubs, ähnliche Farben zu verwenden.

light
luz
lumière
licht

MUCH OF THE FLAIR OF HOTEL ARCHITECTURE is related to the sensitivity with which light is managed in a space to make the design unique. Playing with different qualities, clarities and degrees of natural and artificial light allows scenic and comfortable atmospheres to be created, a must in a hotel project. Light allows for creating, highlighting and delimiting spaces, accenting architectural details and the textures of the materials, as well as embellishing the landscaping.

GRAN PARTE DEL LUCIMIENTO DE LA ARQUITECTURA HOTELERA se relaciona con la sensibilidad con que se ha manejado la luz conforme al diseño del espacio, dándole un sentido particular. Jugar con las distintas calidades, claridades y matices de la luz natural y artificial permite crear atmósferas escenográficas y confortables, imprescindible en el proyecto de un hotel. La iluminación permite precisar, resaltar y delimitar los volúmenes, acentuar los detalles constructivos y las texturas de los materiales, así como embellecer la arquitectura de paisaje.

GRANDE PARTIE DE LA REUSSITE DE L'ARCHITECTURE D'UN HOTEL est liée à la sensibilité avec laquelle a été manipulée la lumière selon le design de l'espace, lui donnant un sens particulier. Jouer avec les différentes qualités, clartés et nuances de la lumière naturelle et artificielle permet de créer des atmosphères esthétiques et confortables, primordiales dans les projets d'hôtel. L'éclairage permettra de préciser, faire ressortir et délimiter les volumes, accentuer les détails et les textures des matériaux, ainsi que d'embellir la vue du paysage.

TEIL DER GROßARTIGKEIT DER HOTELARCHITEKTUR liegt bei der Empfindsamkeit, mit der das Licht, dem Raumentwurf gemäß, benutzt wurde, was ihm eine spezielle Bedeutung gab. Beim Spiel mit den verschiedenen Eigenschaften, Helligkeiten und Schattierungen des natürlichen und künstlichen Lichtes kann man bühnenbildmäßige und gemütliche Atmosphären schaffen, die bei Hotelprojekten unerlässlich sind. Die Beleuchtung kann die Rauminhalte genau bestimmen, hervorheben und begrenzen, so wie auch die Einzelheiten der Materialtexturen unterstreichen und die Landschaftsarchitektur verschönern.

hotels
hoteles
hôtels
hotels

THE EXTERIOR AND INTERIOR LIGHTING OF A HOTEL helps to define and evoke aspects of its image, and its proper design allows the guest to become acquainted with spaces with which he was previously unfamiliar, and to integrate them into his experience; it is thus key that the light in common areas meets the needs of different groups of users.

LA ILUMINACIÓN EXTERIOR E INTERIOR DE UN HOTEL ayuda a precisar y sugerir aspectos de su imagen, pero su buen diseño permite que el huésped se familiarice con espacios antes desconocidos para él y que los pueda hacer parte de su vivencia; por ello es primordial que la luz de las áreas para uso común pueda satisfacer las necesidades de grupos de usuarios y no de uno en particular, lo que sugiere un proyecto en el que la calidad luminosa facilite la visibilidad.

L'ECLAIRAGE EXTERIEUR OU INTERIEUR D'UN HOTEL aide à préciser et à suggérer des aspects de son image, et un design réussi permet que l'hôte se familiarise avec des espaces qui lui étaient avant inconnus ; il est donc essentiel que la lumière des aires collectives puisse satisfaire les besoins de la plupart des usagers, d'où la recherche d'un projet dans lequel la qualité de la lumière favorise la visibilité.

DIE AUßEN UND INNENBELEUCHTUNG EINES HOTELS hilft die Aspekte seines Image genau zu bestimmen und nahezulegen. So ermöglicht es ein guter Entwurf dem Gast auch, Räume kennenzulernen, die ihm fremd waren. Wobei es wesentlich ist, dass das Licht in Gemeinschaftsbereichen die Bedürfnisse von Benutzergruppen befriedigt und nicht nur die eines Einzelen. Weshalb sich ein Projekt empfiehlt, bei dem die Eigenschaften des Lichtes die Sichtbarkeit stärken.

In the living areas and the bars and restaurants of a hotel, it is best that light has a visual presence, making its movement known and highlighting shadows.

En las zonas de estar, en los bares y en los comedores de un hotel conviene que la iluminación tenga un sentido plástico, haciendo notar su movimiento y resaltar las sombras.

Il est recommandé de créer un éclairage esthétique dans les salons, bars et salles à manger d'un hôtel, afin de faire ressortir mouvements et ombres.

In den Aufenthaltsbereichen, Bars und Speisesäalen eines Hotels empfiehlt sich eine mehr plastische Beleuchtung, die Bewegung zeigt und Schatten hervorhebt.

A solution for creating lattices is to use transparent materials that allow light to enter and be used as a decorative option. The more transparent the material, the stronger the connection between the interior and the exterior and the flow of light. But interesting effects can also be attained with translucent and opaque materials such as etched glass or materials like onyx, because they reflect light, bring out shapes, create shadows that cut light from behind, and turn into attractive sources of light.

Una solución para crear cerramientos es utilizar materiales transparentes que permitan el paso de la luz y su aprovechamiento como opción decorativa. Cuanto más transparente sea el material usado, más fuerte será la conexión entre interior y exterior y el flujo de la luz será mayor. Pero también con los materiales translúcidos y opacos como los vidrios esmerilados o materiales como el onix se logran efectos interesantes, pues éstos difuminan la luminosidad, recalcan las formas, permiten percibir las sombras que cortan la luz en el lado posterior y se convierten en atractivas lámparas.

L'une des solutions pour créer des séparations est d'utiliser des matériaux transparents qui permettent le passage de la lumière, en ajoutant une touche décorative. Plus le matériel est transparent, plus la relation entre l'intérieur et l'extérieur est forte et la lumière est présente. Les matériaux translucides et opaques comme les verres dépolis ou les matériaux tels que l'onyx donnent des effets intéressants, ils diffusent la luminosité, soulignent les formes, permettent de percevoir les ombres provenant de l'arrière, et se convertissent en émetteurs de lumière.

Eine Lösung zum Schaffen von Raumhüllen, ist die Verwendung von transparenten Materialien, die das Licht durchlassen und dekorativ zu nutzen sind. Um so transparenter das Material, um so stärker ist die Verbindung zwischen Innen und Außen und um zu größer der Lichtfluss. Aber auch mit transluziden und opaken Materialien, wie etwas Mattgläser oder auch Onyx, lassen sich interessante Effekte produzieren, da sie die Leuchtkraft streuen, Formen unterstreichen, Schatten deutlich machen, die das Licht im Hintergrund schneiden und zu attraktiven Lampen werden.

The reflection of light in mirrors and sleek and polished surfaces such as glass and walls with clear finishes is a part of lighting design.

Forman parte del diseño de iluminación los reflejos de la luz sobre los espejos y otras superficies lisas y pulidas como son los vidrios y los muros terminados en colores claros.

Les reflets de la lumière sur les miroirs et autres surfaces lisses et polies comme le verre et les murs de couleurs claires, font partie d'un projet d'éclairage.

Der Widerschein des Lichtes von Spiegeln und anderen glatten Oberflächen, wie Glas und mit hellen Farben bestrichene Wände sind Bestandteil des Beleuchtungsentwurfs.

When it is evident that a space will be exposed to natural light, it is best to take advantage of the effects resulting from its movement throughout the day. This invites us to think of a rich combination of textures, a play of volumes that creates games of light and shadow, elements with silhouettes that generate shadows and reflections, as well as the color palette given to the walls, ceilings and floors, because color will support and enhance the effects of light on the surfaces.

Cuando se sabe que un espacio estará en contacto con la luz natural es conveniente sacar partido de los efectos que se crearán a causa de los movimientos que ésta tendrá a lo largo del día. Ello invita a pensar en una rica mezcla de texturas, en un juego de volúmenes que provoquen claroscuros, en elementos cuyas siluetas generen sombras y reflejos, así como en la tonalidad que se dé a los muros, techos y pisos, pues el color apoyará y dramatizará los efectos de la luz sobre las superficies.

Sachant qu'un espace va être en contact avec la lumière naturelle, il convient de profiter des effets créés par son mouvement au cours de la journée. Cela invite à penser à un riche mélange de textures, à un jeu de volumes qui provoque des clairs-obscurs, à des éléments dont les silhouettes génèrent des ombres et des reflets, ainsi qu'à la couleur des murs, toits et sols, puisqu'elle appuie et augmente les effets de la lumière sur les surfaces.

Bei einem Raum in Kontakt mit natürlichem Licht, empfiehlt es sich, die Effekte auszunutzen, die dessen Bewegung während des Tagesablaufs schafft. Dies lädt dazu ein, eine reichhaltige Mischung von Texturen einzusetzen, in einem Spiel mit den Rauminhalten, das Helldunkel bringt, in Elementen, deren Umrisse Schatten und Widerscheine produzieren, wie auch in den Tönen der Wände, Decken und Böden, da die Farbe die Effekte des Lichtes auf diesen Flächen unterstützt und dramatisiert.

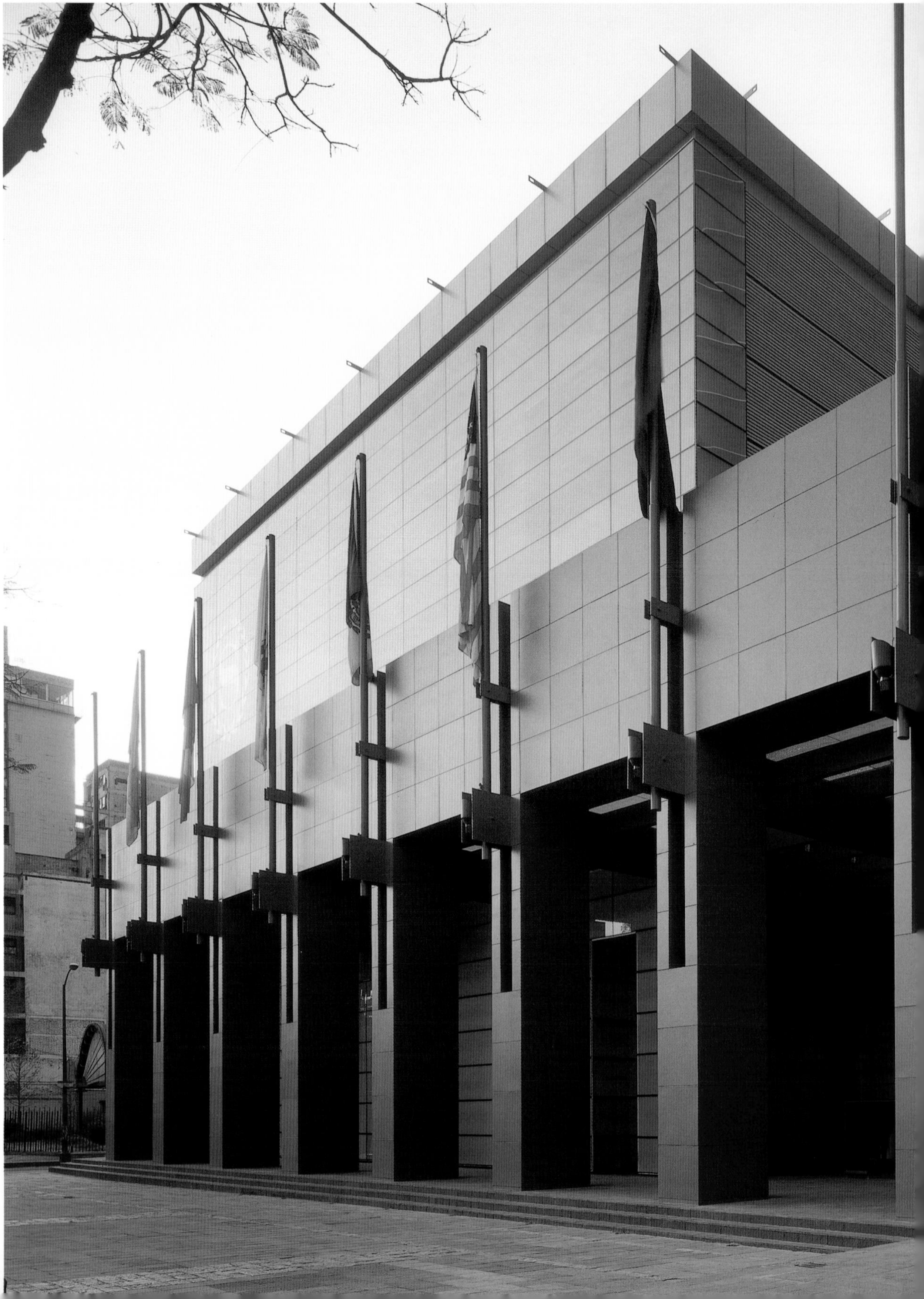

offices
oficinas
bureaux
büroräue

LIGHT HAS A HUGE IMPACT on work. Office lighting must respond to the function and comfort of the space, without losing its ability to mold the ambiance. Nevertheless, not every area in an office requires the same degree of light. In the traffic spaces where no work is carried out, for example, downward lighting from light fixtures with low energy consumption concealed in ceiling tiles can be suitable and aesthetic.

UN ASPECTO DE GRAN IMPACTO en las áreas de trabajo es la luz. La iluminación de oficinas debe responder cualitativamente al funcionamiento y al confort del espacio, sin por ello perder sus posibilidades de modelación del ambiente. No obstante, es obvio que no todas las zonas de una oficina requieren de la misma graduación de luz. En las áreas de circulación donde no se llevan a cabo funciones de trabajo, por ejemplo, puede resultar adecuada y estética, la luz descendente oculta al interior de plafones con luminarias de bajo consumo de electricidad.

L'UN DES ASPECTS IMPORTANTS à considérer sur un lieu de travail est la lumière. L'éclairage des bureaux doit répondre au fonctionnement et au confort de l'espace, sans en perdre ses vertus esthétiques. Il est cependant évident que toutes les aires d'un bureau n'ont pas besoin de la même intensité de lumière. Dans les lieux de passage où l'on ne mène pas de tâches critiques, un éclairage descendant caché à l'intérieur des plafonds avec des luminaires à basse consommation, est adéquat et esthétique.

DAS LICHT IST EIN SEHR EINFLUSSREICHER Gesichtspunkt beim Arbeiten. Die Beleuchtung von Büroräumen muss qualitativ der Arbeitsweise und Bequemlichkeit des Raumes entsprechen, ohne deshalb die Möglichkeit der Gestaltung eines Ambientes zu verhindern. Allerdings ist es klar, dass nicht alle Bürobereiche die gleiche Lichtstärke brauchen. In Verkehrszonen, wo keine Arbeitsfunktionen ausgeübt werden, kann sich zum Beispiel ein absteigendes, in der Decke verstecktes, energiesparendes Licht als geeignet und ästhetisch erweisen.

THE GENERAL LIGHTING of hallways and office entrances can be designed in different ways, though it is better that it is sharp and semi-direct, focusing the flow of light at the floor and having it reflect off the ceiling and walls. An alternative is to follow the contours of the ceiling tiles by concealing fluorescent light fixtures in them; another is to embed halogen light units at regular intervals.

LA ILUMINACIÓN GENERAL de pasillos y accesos de oficinas puede ser diseñada de muy diversas maneras aunque es preferible que su luz sea nítida y semi-directa, haciendo que el flujo luminoso se dirija hacia el suelo y se refleje en el techo y las paredes. Una alternativa es seguir el contorno de plafones encubriendo dentro de éstos lámparas de tipo fluorescente; otra es empotrar unidades de luces de halógeno dispuestas en intervalos.

L'ÉCLAIRAGE GENERAL des couloirs de bureaux peut être conçu de manières très différentes bien qu'il est préférable que sa lumière soit limpide et indirecte, on peut orienter le flux lumineux vers le sol et créer des reflets sur murs et plafonds, en suivant leur contour et en y disposant des lampes de type fluorescent ; on peut aussi encastrer à intervalles réguliers, des éléments de lumière halogènes.

DIE ALLGEMEINBELEUCHTUNG von Fluren und Büroeingängen kann auf viele verschiedene Weisen entworfen werden, obwohl es sich empfiehlt, dass ihr Licht klar und halbdirekt sein sollte, wobei die Lichtflut sich auf den Boden richtet und von Decke und Wänden zurückstrahlt. Eine Alternative folgt der Deckenkontur, in der man Leuchtgaslampen versteckt, die andere lässt dort in Intervallen angeordnete Halogenlichteinheiten ein.

There are spaces where the presence of natural light is of vital importance, such as in studios for painting and sculpting; there, formal architectural elements such as domes, skylights, and large windows turn into powerful captivators of natural light, blurring the frontier between interior and exterior. Architecturally, there placement, combined with the change in light throughout the day, makes it possible to use the timeless beauty of games of light and shadow, allowing their sequences to alternate when any of them is extended, reduced, deepened, advanced, or diminished. This way, light and shadow are protagonists in the design and help to create a magnificent work environment.

Hay recintos donde la precencia de la luz natural es de vital importancia, como en los talleres de pintura y de escultura, ahi los elementos arquitectónicos formales, como domos, claraboyas, ventanales y tragaluces se convierten en potentes captadores de luz natural, disipando la frontera entre interior y exterior. Arquitectónicamente su ubicación, aunada a los cambios de la luz durante el día, hace posible contar con la inagotable belleza de los claroscuros, permitiendo que las secuencias de luz y sombra se alternen. De esta forma, luz y sombra protagonizan el diseño y contribuyen a crear una magnifica atmósfera de trabajo.

Dans certains espaces,comme les ateliers de peinture et de sculpture, la présence de la lumière naturelle est primordiale et des éléments architecturaux comme les dômes, vasistas, baies vitrées et lucarnes se convertissent en de puissants capteurs de lumière naturelle, dissipant la frontière entre l'intérieur et l'extérieur. Dans l'architecture, leur place, ajoutée à l'évolution de la lumière au cours de la journée, permet de profiter de la beauté des clairs-obscurs, et que les séquences d'ombre et de lumière s'alternent, et jouent ainsi le premier rôle, créant d'excellentes conditions de travail.

Es gibt Räume, wo die Gegenwart von natürlichem Licht von größter Bedeutung ist, wie etwa Maler- und Bildhaueraliers, wo formale architektonische Elemente, wie Kuppeln, Oberlichter, Großfenster und Luken zu kräftigen Quellen des natürlichen Lichts werden, die die Grenze zwischen Innen und Außen verwischen. Ihre Anordnung in der Architektur, zusammen mit dem Lichtwechsel während des Tages, ermöglichen eine immer neue Schönheit von Helldunkeln, die es Licht und Schatten erlaubt sich abzuwechseln und auf diese Weise zu Hauptdarstellern des Entwurfs zu werden und zur Schöpfung einer großartigen Arbeitsatmosphäre beizutragen.

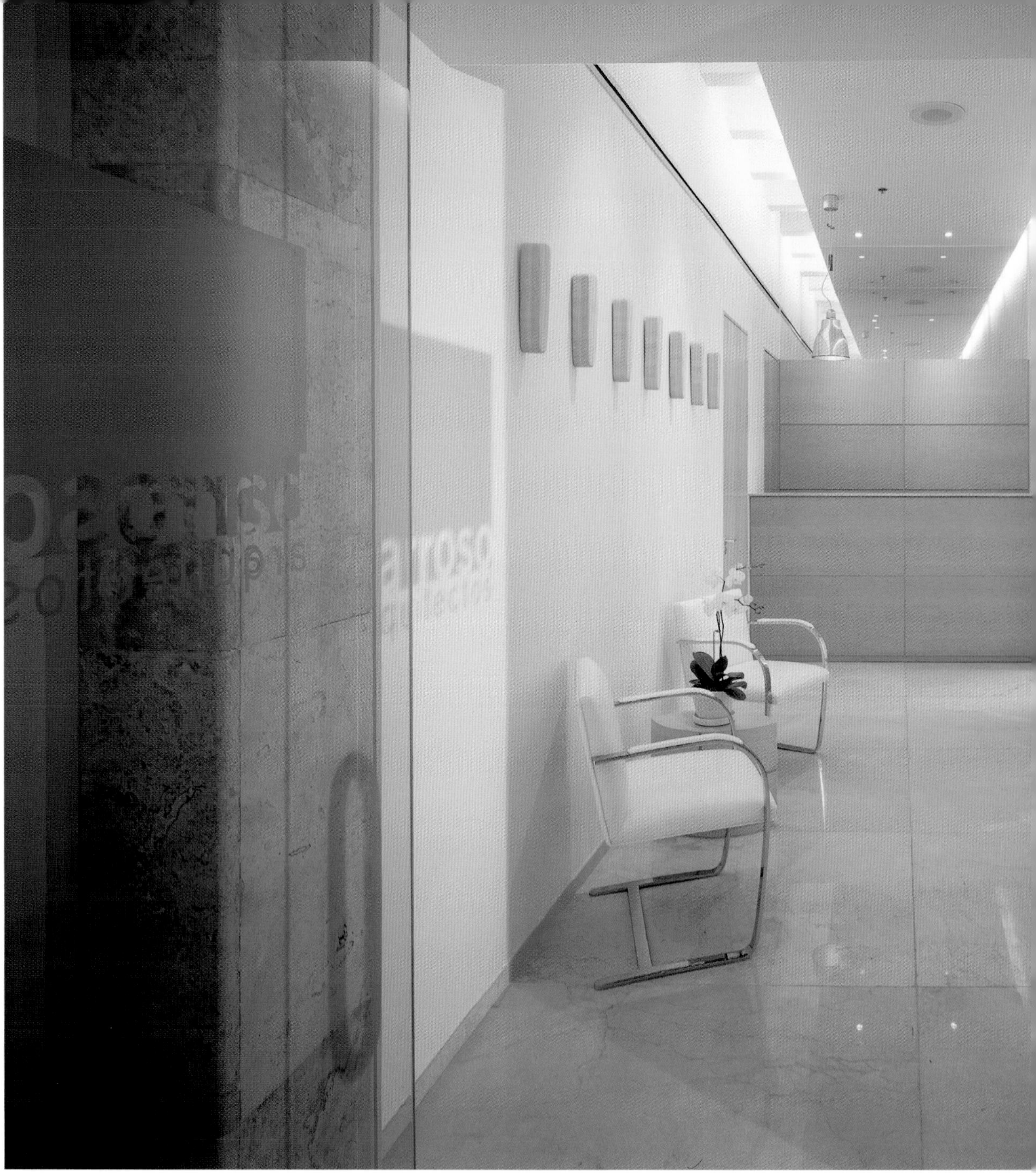

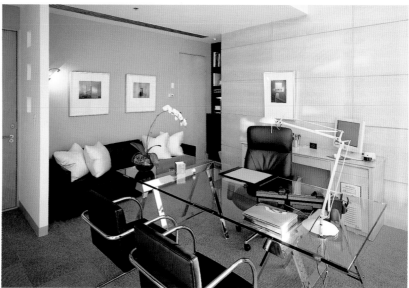

The different qualities and colors of light can become a design instrument if used as guides for differentiating and defining spaces, allowing light and its changes to suggest the idea of continuity or the limits of an area, to indicate a path or direction to follow, or where to stand.

Las distintas calidades y colores de la luz pueden convertirse en un instrumento de diseño si se les utiliza como guías para diferenciar y definir espacios, logrando que sea la luz y sus cambios los que sugieran la idea de continuidad o límite de un área, indiquen un recorrido o una dirección hacia la cual seguir.

Les différentes qualités et couleurs de la lumière peuvent
se convertir en un instrument de design si on les utilise pour
différencier et définir les espaces, grâce à la lumière et ses
changements qui suggèrent une idée de continuité, de
limite ou indique une direction à suivre.

Die Eigenschaften und Farben des Lichtes können zum
Entwurfsinstrument werden, wenn man sie als Richtlinie zum
Differenzieren und Definieren von Räumen benutzt, wobei
das Licht und sein Wechseln das Gefühl von Kontinuität oder
Trennung des Raumes bewirken und den Weg oder die
Richtung weisen für die Fortbewegung oder das Bleiben.

So-called transition spaces don't have to be thought of as being merely functional, small and uninteresting areas; to the contrary, they can be used as areas with an agreeable volume composition with a lighting design with its own decorative weight, but which also allows for bringing out the three-dimensional shapes, textures and colors of the different materials, as well as specific details, whether works of art or simply decorative objects.

Los lugares llamados de transición no tienen que ser considerados en la tipología de oficinas como meramente funcionales, de dimensiones reducidas y como áreas sin mayor interés; por el contrario, pueden ser aprovechados como zonas de agradables composiciones volumétricas que cuenten con un diseño de iluminación que por sí mismo tenga un peso decorativo, pero que también permita que se destaquen las formas tridimensionales, las texturas y colores de los diversos materiales, así como algunos detalles específicos, ya sea que se trate de piezas de arte u objetos simplemente ornamentales.

Les lieux de transition ne doivent pas uniquement être considérés dans la typologie des bureaux sous des aspects fonctionnels, de dimensions réduites et comme des aires sans grand intérêt; au contraire, on peut en faire des zones agréables avec des compositions volumétriques et un éclairage décoratif, qui permet aussi de faire ressortir les volumes, les textures et couleurs des matériaux, ainsi que certains détails particuliers, comme des oeuvres d'art ou de simples objets ornementaux.

Sogenannte Übergangsbereiche müssen in der Typologie der Büroräume nicht nur als funktionelle, kleinräumige, uninteressante Zonen betrachtet werden, sondern sollten sie, ganz im Gegenteil, als Bereiche angenehmer inhaltlicher Kompositionen genutzt werden, mit einem Beleuchtungsentwurf, der selbst ein dekoratives Gewicht bringt, aber es auch erlaubt dreidimensionale Formen, Texturen und Farben der verschiedenen Materialien, sowie einige spezielle Einzelheiten hervorzuheben, wie Kunstgegenstände oder einfach dekorative Objekte.

Luminosity and the feeling of space is ensured in offices with few pieces of furniture with pure line and simple shapes, minimum decorative objects and where there is widespread use of white on walls, ceilings and floors. If metal details, transparencies and sleek, polished surfaces are added, the glimmers and reflection created by the effects of light upon them will grant the space unique aesthetic and clean qualities.

En aquellas oficinas en las que se incluyen pocos muebles de líneas puras y formas sencillas, un mínimo de objetos decorativos, y se hace uso generalizado del color blanco en muros, techos y pisos, se asegura la luminosidad y la sensación de amplitud del espacio. Si además existen detalles metálicos, transparencias y superficies con acabados lisos y bien pulidos, los brillos y los reflejos provocados por la acción de la luz sobre ellos, le conferirán al espacio cualidades estéticas y de limpieza únicas.

Dans les bureaux avec peu de meubles de lignes pures et formes simples, avec un minimum d'objets décoratifs et avec du blanc sur tous les murs, les plafonds et les sols on assure la luminosité et une sensation d'amplitude de l'espace. Si en plus, on ajoute certains détails métalliques, des transparences et des surfaces aux finitions lisses et polies, les reflets provoqués par l'action de la lumière confèrent à l'espace des qualités esthétiques et de pureté uniques.

In Büroräumen, in denen wenige Möbel mit klaren Linien und einfachen Formen, eine Mindestanzahl von Dekorobjekten und die Farbe Weiß für Wände, Decken und Böden eingeführt werden, sichert man Leuchtkraft und Weiträumigkeit. Wenn dazu noch einige metallene Einzelheiten, Transparenzmaterialien und Oberflächen mit glatter oder gut pullierter Endbehandlung und Glanz und Widerschein des Lichtes auf ihnen existieren, dann schenken sie dem Raum einzigartige Eigenschaften von Ästhetik und Sauberkeit.

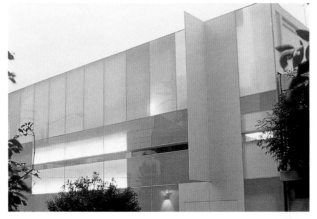

Light and shadow help to bring out
and define relief in architectural
details and the textures of the
building materials.

La luz y la sombra ayudan a resaltar y
a ponderar los relieves de los detalles
constructivos y las texturas de los
materiales de construcción.

La lumière et l'ombre aident à faire
ressortir et à pondérer les reliefs et les
textures des matériaux de construction.

Licht und Schatten ermöglichen es,
die Reliefs der baulichen Einzelheiten
und die Texturen der Baustoffe zu
unterstreichen und hervorzuheben.

Establishing relationships between the interior and exterior spaces using large windows allows for capturing generous amounts of light and favors natural ventilation. However, often these entrances for light must be regulated with formal architectural elements such as low walls, beams, rafters or a horizontal transom, or else with meshes, pergolas, blinds and drapes, because they can be an irritation when working. When this occurs, these elements must fulfill a double role: aesthetic and functional.

Establecer relaciones entre los espacios interiores y los exteriores a través de grandes ventanales permite, además, que sean captadas generosas cantidades de luz y que se favorezca la ventilación natural. Sin embargo, en muchas ocasiones estas entradas luminosas tienen que ser reguladas con algunos elementos arquitectónicos formales del tipo de muretes, vigas, listones y otros travesaños horizontales, o bien con mallas, pérgolas, persianas y cortinajes, debido a que pueden resultar incómodas para realizar actividades laborales. Cuando así ocurre, se debe procurar que estos elementos cumplan con una doble misión: estética y funcional.

Mettre en relation les espaces intérieurs et extérieurs à travers de grandes baies vitrées permet de capter de généreuses quantités de lumière et de favoriser la ventilation naturelle. La plupart du temps, ces entrées de lumière doivent être régulées avec des éléments architecturaux formels tels que des murets, des poutres et autres éléments horizontaux, alors que les grilles, pergolas, volets et rideaux peuvent être incommodes pour travailler. Dans ce cas, il faudra faire en sorte que ces éléments accomplissent une mission esthétique et fonctionnelle.

Das Schaffen von Beziehungen zwischen Innen- und Außenräumen durch große Fenster, ermöglicht einen besseren Lichteinfall und fördert die natürliche Lüftung. Oft allerdings, müssen diese Lichteinlässe mit formalen architektonischen Elementen, wie Niedrigwände, Träger, Leisten und andere horizontale Querbalken reguliert werden oder auch mit Netzgeweben, Pergolas, Jalousien und Vorhängen, da sie die bequeme Ausübung der Tätigkeiten stören können. Wenn das geschieht, ist es möglich diese Elemente zweifach zu nutzen, sowohl ästhetisch, wie auch funktionell.

Although some people prefer that office lighting is very bright and comes from fluorescent lighting, others lean towards warm lighting that is in harmony with the decoration.

Establecer relaciones entre los espacios interiores y los exteriores a través de grandes ventanales permite captar generosas cantidades de luz y que se favorezca la ventilación natural.

Créer des relations entre les espaces intérieurs et extérieurs avec de grandes baies vitrées permet de capter de généreuses quantités de lumière et favorise la ventilation naturelle.

Das Schaffen von Beziehungen zwischen Innen- und Außenräumen durch große Fenster ermöglicht einen großzügigen Lichteinfall und fördert die natürliche Lüftung.

Embedded light fixtures aimed at the floor focus on a limited space, and thus they are not an option for general lighting.

Las luminarias colgadas con luz descendente y concentrada, focalizan su acción sobre un espacio limitado, por lo que no son una opción como iluminación general.

Pour l'éclairage général, les luminaires encastrés, dont les faisceaux descendants et concentrés agissent sur des surfaces réduites, ne sont pas adéquats.

Eingelassene Beleuchtungskörper mit absteigendem gezieltem Licht dienen nicht zur allgemeinen Beleuchtung, da sie ihre Aktivität auf begrenzte Räume richten.

When the façades of a building are covered by large amounts of glass, the exchange of light between the interior and the exterior becomes dynamic and depends on the passage of the day. Natural daylight positively affects the atmosphere of the interior as much as the light from the interior also has important consequences on the exterior at night. The layout, quantity and dimensions of the walls play an essential role in this exchange and determine how the building relates to the urban environment.

Cuando grandes cantidades de vidrio cubren las fachadas de una construcción, el intercambio de luz entre el interior y el exterior se vuelve dinámico y dependiente del transcurrir del día. La luz natural diurna afecta positivamente el ambiente interior en tanto que la proveniente del interior tiene a su vez importantes consecuencias por la noche sobre el exterior. La disposición, cantidad y las dimensiones de las ventanas juegan un papel esencial en este intercambio y determinan la manera en la que el edificio se relaciona con el entorno urbano.

Lorsque de grandes quantités de verre couvrent les façades d'une construction, l'échange de lumière entre l'intérieur et l'extérieur devient dynamique et dépend de la lumière du jour. La lumière naturelle diurne affecte positivement l'ambiance intérieure et celle qui provient de l'intérieur porte d'importantes conséquences sur l'extérieur la nuit. La disposition, la quantité et les dimensions des fenêtres jouent un rôle essentiel dans cet échange et déterminent la manière dont la construction est mise en relation avec son entourage urbain.

Wenn große Mengen von Glas die Fassaden eines Gebäudes bedecken, wird der Lichtaustausch zwischen Innen und Außen dynamisch und abhängig vom Tagesablauf. Das natürliche Tageslicht beeinflusst das Ambiente im Inneren günstig, während das von Innen kommende Licht, des Nachts bedeutende Folgen für Außen hat. Die Verteilung, Menge und Maße der Fenster spielen eine wesentliche Rolle bei diesem Austausch und bestimmen die Art der Beziehung des Gebäudes mit der städtischen Umgebung.

The fading afternoon light multiplies the effects of shadows on the solid elements of a building, while the reflections of the lighting used at night copy the images on glazed surfaces.

La luz rasante del atardecer multiplica los efectos de las sombras sobre las partes sólidas de una construcción, en tanto que los reflejos de la luz nocturna desdoblan las imágenes sobre las superficies acristaladas.

La lumière rasante du crépuscule multiplie les effets des ombres sur les parties solides d'une construction, si bien que les reflets de la lumière nocturne dédoublent les images sur les surfaces de verre.

Die rasante Beleuchtung der Abendröte vervielfältigt die Schatteneffekte auf den festen Teilen des Bauwerks, während die Widerscheine des nächtlichen Lichtes die Bilder auf den gläsernen Oberflächen verdoppeln.

Generally, in a minimalist environment there are some elements which draw attention. They can include certain works of art, particularly sculptures, although they can also include other three-dimensional figures, which become sublime revelations when they received focused lighting, and earn a leading role in the design. The technique of focused and accented lighting that suits these pieces is achieved with halogen light fixtures that have a wide range of degrees, allowing for accurate optical control, illuminating objects with the minimum loss of light and using energy efficiently.

En un ambiente minimalista generalmente existen algunos elementos en los que se concentra la atención. Algunas piezas de arte, especialmente las esculturas, aunque puede ocurrir con otros tridimensionales, se convierten en revelaciones sublimes al ser iluminadas puntualmente, al tiempo que adquieren un protagonismo en el diseño. La técnica de iluminación que por lo común se utiliza para destacar la presencia de estos objetos, es la focalizada y consiste en centrar la fuente de luz sobre ellos, otra opción es un baño de luz uniforme sobre toda la superficie donde se ubican.

Dans une ambiance minimaliste, il existe généralement certains éléments sur lesquels on centre l'attention. Certaines œuvres d'art, en particulier les sculptures ou autres éléments tridimensionnels, deviennent des révélations sublimes si elles sont illuminées ponctuellement, et prennent une importance majeure dans la décoration. La technique d'éclairage qui s'utilise pour faire ressortir la présence de ces objets est la focalisation et consiste à centrer la source de lumière directement sur eux, on peut aussi avoir recours à un bain de lumière uniforme sur toute la surface où ils se trouvent.

In einem minimalistischen Ambiente existieren meist einige Elemente, die die Aufmerksamkeit aufsichziehen. Manche Kunstgegenstände, vor allem Skulpturen, obwohl es auch bei anderen dreidimensionellen geschehen kann, werden durch Punktbeleuchtung zu sublimen Offenbarungen und zugleich zum Hauptdarsteller des Entwurfs. Die gezielte Beleuchtung ist die meistverwendete Methode zum Hervorheben dieser Objekte. Sie besteht daraus eine Lichtquelle konkret auf sie zu richten, während eine weitere das einheitliche mit-Licht-Umfluten der ganzen Fläche, auf der es sich befindet, ist.

Natural light is most valued when in comes to lighting, but its constant changes make it difficult to manipulate in the interior space under established paradigms. This is because several factors influence its behavior, such as the orientation of the space, shadows from other buildings, the colors and finishes of the walls, the proportion and size of the windows, and the season of the year... Therefore, only an in-site assessment throughout the day will inform us of its movement and help us to find the proper solution for the artificial lighting that will accompany it.

La luz natural es la más preciada de iluminación, pero sus constantes cambios dificultan manipularla en el espacio interior bajo paradigmas establecidos. Ello ocurre porque en su comportamiento influyen múltiples factores como la orientación del espacio, las sombras de otras construcciones, los colores y acabados de los muros, la proporción y dimensión de las ventanas, la estación del año... Por eso, sólo el estudio in situ durante las distintas horas del día permitirá conocer sus directrices y encontrar la solución adecuada para la iluminación artificial que la acompañará.

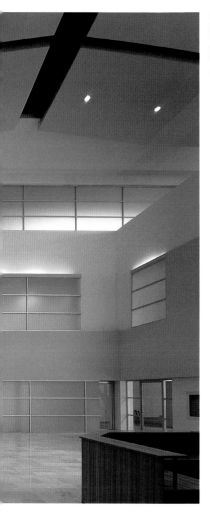

La lumière naturelle est la plus appréciée, mais ses changements constants rendent difficile sa manipulation selon des règles établies. Dans son comportement jouent de multiples facteurs comme l'orientation de l'espace, les ombres d'autres constructions, les couleurs et finitions des murs, la proportion et dimension des fenêtres, la saison... C'est pourquoi, son étude in situ à différentes heures de la journée permettra de connaître les directions qu'elle peut prendre et de trouver la solution adéquate pour l'éclairage artificiel qui l'accompagne.

Das natürliche Licht ist als Beleuchtung das meist geschätzte, allerdings machen seine ständigen Wechsel das Handhaben im Inneren unter festgelegten Paradigmen schwierig, weil sein Verhalten durch mehrere Faktoren beeinflusst wird, wie etwa die Ausrichtung des Raumes, die Schatten anderer Bauwerke, die Farben und Oberflächen der Wände, die Prop ortionen und Maße der Fenster, die Jahreszeit... Aus diesem Grund ist die Untersuchung vor Ort zu verschiedenen Tageszeiten unerlässlich, um die Richtlinien und die geeignete Lösung für die dazupassende künstliche Beleuchtung zu finden.

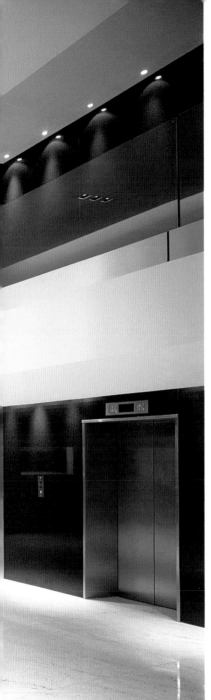

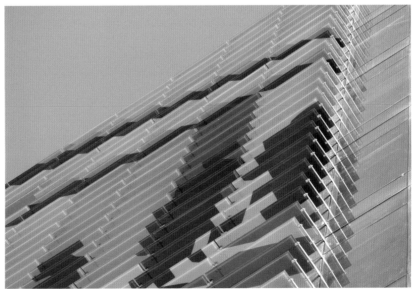

restaurants   restaurantes   restaurants   restaurants

CAREFUL LIGHTING may be one of the most attractive aspects for the clientele of a restaurant, inviting them to linger. The color of the light plays, in this sense, a fundamental role. Even though the selection of the color palette of the lighting depends on the particular characteristics of each place, it is preferable that the warm atmospheres created by amber, yellow and soft white, prevail in a restaurant.

UNA ILUMINACIÓN BIEN CUIDADA puede ser uno de los aspectos que más atraiga a la clientela de un restaurante y la invite a permanecer en él. El color de la luz tiene, en este sentido, un papel fundamental. Aunque la elección de los tonos de la iluminación depende de las características particulares de cada sitio, es preferible que en restaurantes dominen las atmósferas cálidas provenientes de las tonalidades de luz ámbar, amarillo y blanco cálido.

UN ECLAIRAGE SOIGNE peut être l'un des aspects qui attire le plus la clientèle d'un restaurant et l'invite à y rester. La couleur de la lumière a, dans ce sens, un rôle fondamental. Bien que le choix des tons de l'éclairage dépend des caractéristiques particulières de chaque lieu, il est préférable que dans des restaurants dominent les atmosphères chaleureuses provenant des tonalités de lumière ambre, jaune et blanche.

varied spaces
espacios diversos
espaces divers
allerlei räume

EINE SORGFÄLTIG GEPLANTE Beleuchtung kann zu einem der einladensten Aspekte für die Gäste eines Restaurants werden, damit sie dort verweilen wollen. Die Farbe des Lichtes ist in diesem Sinn von grundlegender Bedeutung. Wenn auch die Wahl der Farbtöne für die Beleuchtung von den jeweiligen Eigenschaften eines jeden Raumes abhängt, ist es für Restaurants ratsam, warme Atmosphären aus Amber-, Gelb- oder Weißtönen vorzuziehen.

WHEN LIGHTING RESTAURANTS that do not have entrances for natural light, as well as their scenery, it is valid to use to the technical means at hand in order to surprise. Artificial lighting with alternating light and dark areas will always capture the attention of diners. To enhance said effect, intensely polished metals can be used on some details of the architecture and furniture, creating linear reflections or rugged surfaces that reflect light in every direction.

EN LA ILUMINACIÓN DE RESTAURANTES que no cuentan con entradas de luz natural, así como en la escenografía, es válido utilizar los medios técnicos al alcance para sorprender gratamente. Una iluminación artificial en la que se alternan sabiamente zonas claras y oscuras siempre atrapará la contemplación del comensal. Para acrecentar los efectos se pueden emplear metales muy pulidos en algunos detalles de la arquitectura y el mobiliario provocando destellos lineales, o superficies rugosas que reflejen la luz en todas direcciones.

DANS L'ECLAIRAGE DE RESTAURANTS qui n'ont pas d'entrées de lumière naturelle, on peut employer des moyens techniques surprenants. Un éclairage artificiel dans lequel on alterne subtilement des zones claires et obscures attirera toujours l'attention du client. Pour augmenter les effets on peut avoir recours à des métaux très lisses pour certains détails de l'architecture et le mobilier provoquant des reflets linéaires, ou des surfaces rugueuses qui reflètent la lumière dans toutes les directions.

BEI DER BELEUCHTUNG VON RESTAURANTS ohne natürliche Lichteinfälle, wie auch bei Bühnenbildern, können technische Mittel genutzt werden, um zu überraschen. Eine künstliche Beleuchtung, bei der sich helle und dunkle Zonen abwechseln, fesselt immer die Aufmerksamkeit der Gäste. Um diese Effekte zu stärken, können auf Glanz pullierte Metalle in einem Architekturdetail und beim Mobiliar eingesetzt werden, die lineare Lichtblitze erzeugen oder unebene Oberflächen, die das Licht in alle Richtungen widerspiegeln.

To illuminate the dining area of a restaurant, it is acceptable to use several techniques. It is best that the general lighting is even, it might be embedded in the perimeter of the ceiling tiles or with lines of light, preferably halogen, placed at regular intervals. Environmental lighting is achieved by hanging lamps above the tables; focused lighting will be related to the objects or elements intended to be highlighted.

Para iluminar el comedor de un restaurante es aceptable valerse de varios tipos de técnicas. Conviene que la iluminación general sea pareja, puede ser empotrada en el plafón perimetralmente o con líneas de luz, preferentemente halógenas, colocadas en intervalos regulares. La iluminación ambiental se podrá lograr con lámparas colgantes haces de luz concentrados hacia las mesas; en tanto que la iluminación puntual tendrá que ver con los objetos o elementos que se desee destacar, dirigiendo hacia ellos una luz de control óptico preciso o incluso convirtiendo el objeto mínimo en una lámpara.

Pour éclairer la salle à manger d'un restaurant plusieurs techniques peuvent être envisagées. L'éclairage général doit être homogène, il peut être encastré dans le périmètre d'un plafond ou placé en ligne, en préférant les halogènes, placés à des intervalles réguliers. L'éclairage d'ambiance pourra s'obtenir avec des lampes suspendues et des lumières de faisceaux concentrés vers les tables ; si bien que l'éclairage ponctuel servira à mettre des objets ou des éléments en valeur avec une lumière de contrôle optique précis ou même en convertissant le propre objet en une lampe.

Zur Beleuchtung des Speisesaales eines Restaurants dürfen verschiedene Techniken benutzt werden. Es empfiehlt sich, die Allgemeinbeleuchtung gleichmäßig zu gestalten, durch in der Decke eingelassene Umfassungslichter oder Lichterreihen, vor allem, in gleichen Abständen angeordnete Halogenlichter. Die Zentralbeleuchtung kann durch, auf die Tische konzentrierte Hängelampen geschehen, während die gezielte von den Objekten oder Elementen bestimmt wird, die hervorzuheben sind, um Lichtquellen auf sie zu richten, die man genau steuern kann oder sogar das Objekt zur Lampe zu machen.

An always attractive design alternative for public gathering spaces is to capture the light from above through verandas and solariums which sometimes use climatic glazing to allow the free passage of daylight, and other times filter and vary it by placing carvings, slots, piercings, blinds, mullions or fabrics that add to the aesthetics of the space while contributing to its functional side. This option allows the diner to be in touch with the exterior environment and the landscape.

Una alternativa de diseño que siempre resulta atrayente para lugares de reunión, es la captación de luz cenital a través de verandas y solarios que unas veces utilizan vidrios climáticos y dejan libre la incidencia de la luz solar, y otras la filtran y tamizan interponiendo calados, rendijas, perforados, persianas, parteluces o telas que, además de cumplir con su parte funcional, contribuyen a la estética del espacio. Esta opción permite al comensal estar en contacto con el ambiente exterior y con el paisaje.

Pour des lieux de réunion, il est intéressant de capter la lumière di soleil à travers des vérandas et solariums de verre thermique et qui laisse libre l'incidence de la lumière naturelle alors que d'autres la filtrent et la tamisent interposant grilles, perforations, volets, meneaux ou tissus qui en plus de leur aspect fonctionnel, apportent à l'esthétique de l'espace. Cette option permet au client d'être en contact avec l'ambiance extérieure et avec le paysage.

Eine immer anziehend wirkende Entwurfsalternative für gemeinschaftliche Treffpunkte, ist der Lichteinfall von oben, durch Verandas und Sonnenterrassen, die manchmal Klimaschutzglas benutzen und den freien Einfall des Sonnenlichtes zulassen und andere Male dieses Filtern und Streuen durch Streifen, Gitter, Durchlöcherungen, Jalousien, Zwischenpfeiler oder Stoffe, die außer ihrer funktionellen Aufgabe dem Raum noch Ästhetik bringen. Diese Lösung ermöglicht dem Gast den Kontakt zur äußeren Umgebung und zur Landschaft.

cafes cafeterias cafés cafés

gyms gimnasios gymnases fitnesszentrer

Gym and club projects must have independent areas for private use, and common areas suitable for team sports. This forces us to think of different types of lighting according to the size and function of each space.

Los proyectos de gimnasios y clubes deben contar con áreas independientes para uso privado y otras comunitarias aptas para realizar algún deporte en colectividad. Esto obliga a pensar en distintos tipos de iluminación de acuerdo con el tamaño de cada espacio y con la función que se realice en él.

Les projets de gymnases et clubs doivent proposer des aires indépendantes à usage privé et d'autres communautaires aptes à la réalisation de sports collectifs. Cela oblige à penser à l'éclairage selon la taille de chaque espace et à l'activité qui s'y réalise.

Bei Projekten für Sportzentren und Clubs müssen Bereiche für private Benutzung geplant werden und andere für gemeinschaftliche, wo Teamsport ausgeübt werden kann. Dies zwingt zum Beachten der verschiedenen Beleuchtungsarten, je nach Größe des Raumes und der dort ausgeübten Aktivitäten.

Ideally, the different exercise rooms will have lighting that goes along with the discipline being practiced in them. Yoga and meditation, for example, are practices that follow slow rhythms; when the spaces in which they are practiced have natural entrances for light, agreeable scenes are produced that help to achieve relaxation.

Es ideal que los distintos salones de ejercicios, cuenten con un alumbrado acorde con la disciplina que en ellos se lleva a cabo. El yoga y la meditación, por ejemplo, son prácticas que siguen ritmos acompasados; cuando los espacios donde se realizan cuentan con entradas de luz natural, ésta produce escenas agradables que cooperan a que se consiga la relajación.

Les salles d'exercice ont besoin d'un éclairage en accord avec la discipline qui y est pratiquée. Le yoga et la méditation, par exemple, requièrent de mouvements qui suivent un rythme régulier ; lorsque les espaces où ils se réalisent ont des entrées de lumière naturelle, on produit des scènes agréables qui contribuent à la relaxation.

Im Idealfall haben die unterschiedlichen Sporträume eine Beleuchtung, die der Ausübung der Sportart entspricht. Yoga und Meditation sind zum Beispiel Übungen die gleichmäßigen Rhythmen folgen. Wenn die Räume, in denen sie ausgeübt werden, natürlichen Lichteinfall aufweisen, dann produziert dieser angenehme Szenen, die die Entspannung fördern.

stores tiendas boutiques läden

THE LIGHTING OF A STORE has an influence on the feelings perceived by the buyer and on his buying experience. It is said that yellowish or clear light helps buyers to relax and stay in the store longer. Some amber colored onyx slabs, which due to their thinness allow light to flow through them, become attractive sources of warm, diffuse light.

LA ILUMINACIÓN DE UNA TIENDA influye en las sensaciones que percibe el consumidor y en su experiencia de compra. Se dice que la luz amarillenta o de tonos pastel ayuda a que los compradores se relajen y permanezcan mayor tiempo en el establecimiento. Algunas placas de ónix que poseen color ámbar y que por su esbeltez permiten que la luz las traspase, se convierten en atractivas fuentes difusoras de luz cálida.

L'ÉCLAIRAGE D'UN MAGASIN influence les sensations perçues par le consommateur dans son expérience d'achat. On dit que la lumière jaune ou de tons pastel aide à ce que les acheteurs se détendent et restent plus longtemps dans l'établissement. Par exemple, des plaques d'onyx de couleur ambre translucides, grâce de leur finesse, deviennent d'attrayantes sources de lumière chaleureuse.

DIE BELEUCHTUNG EINES LADENS beeinflusst die Gefühle, die beim Kunden erweckt werden und dessen Einkaufserlebnis. Es wird gesagt, dass gelbliches oder pastellfarbenes Licht den Einkaufenden helfen, sich zu entspannen und länger im Geschäft zu verweilen. Einige amberfarbene Onyxscheiben, die dank ihrer Dünne das Licht durchlassen, werden zu attraktiven Diffusoren eines warmen Lichtes.

The general characteristics of light fixtures to be installed in a store are determined by the specifics of the store, particularly its height, and the type of products it sells.

Las características generales de las luminarias que se van a instalar en una tienda, se determinan por las particularidades del local, especialmente por su altura física y por el tipo de productos que allí se vendan.

Les caractéristiques des luminaires à installer dans un magasin se déterminent par les particularités du local, notamment par sa hauteur physique, et par le type de produits qui s'y est vendu.

Die Beschaffenheit von in einem Laden zu installierenden Lichtern, wird von den speziellen Eigenschaften des Geschäfts bestimmt, vor allem von der räumlichen Höhe und von den dort angebotenen Produkten.

Displays are tools for attracting the consumer by highlighting the products in a particular space; their design, colors, shape and type of stands are determined by the desired image, but it is best that their lighting stand out and be prioritized with respect to the rest of the store. For this purpose, a soft light can be used as a base, and then some elements can be highlighted with focused lighting using high-pressure sodium light fixtures; the consumer will be attracted by strong lighting on some objects.

Los exhibidores son una herramienta para atraer al consumidor haciendo destacar desde un espacio particular los productos; su diseño, colores, forma y tipo de soportes de exposición se deciden según la imagen deseada, pero conviene que su iluminación se destaque y jerarquice respecto de la del resto de la tienda. Para ello, se puede recurrir a una luz suave como base y subrayar algunos elementos con iluminación focal a través de luminarias de sodio de alta presión; el consumidor se sentirá atraído por los golpes de luz sobre algunos objetos.

Les supports d'exposition comme les rayons, doivent se choisir selon l'image à transmettre et permettent d'attirer le consommateur sur les produits ; leur design, leurs couleurs, et formes, mais il convient que leur éclairage ressorte et hiérarchise le magasin. Pour cela, on peut avoir recours à une lumière douce comme base et souligner certains éléments avec un éclairage concentré à travers des luminaires au sodium à haute pression; le consommateur se sentira attiré par les lumières plus intenses orientées sur certains objets.

Die Schauschränke dienen zum Ansprechen des Verbraucher, in dem sie von einem bestimmten Raum aus Produkte hervorheben. Ihr Entwurf, Farbe, Form und die Art der Ausstellungshilfen werden je nach gewünschtem Image ausgewählt. Jedoch empfiehlt es sich, ihre Beleuchtung zu betonen und in Bezug auf die des restlichen Ladens in eine Rangordnung zu bringen. Dazu dient ein sanftes Licht als Basis und gezielte Natriumhochdruckbeleuchtung zum Unterstreichen von Objekten, wobei der Lichtaufprall auf diese die Aufmerksamkeit des Kunden erweckt.

beauty shops   estéticas   salons de beauté   schönheitssalons

design
diseño

HOTEL DESIGN is comprehensive and specialized; it encompasses public and private areas, and its proper execution contributes, to a great extent, to the success of the hotel. Exteriors are also decisive; there are solutions for all climates, but an interesting alternative is tensile architecture using weather-resistant membranes, in which polyester or glass fibers, coated with Teflon, are stretched between poles.

EL DISEÑO DE HOTELES es integral y especializado, abarca tanto las áreas públicas como las privadas, y de su buena realización depende en gran medida el éxito del hotel. También son determinantes las zonas exteriores, existen soluciones para todo tipo de climas, pero una alternativa interesante es la arquitectura textil de membranas resistentes a la intemperie, cuyas telas de fibras de poliéster o de vidrio, recubiertas con teflón, son tensadas sobre postes.

LE DESIGN D'UN HOTEL est un exercice complet et spécialisé, il comprend les aires publiques ou privées, et de la réussite du projet dépend en grande partie le succès de l'hôtel. L'extérieur est tout aussi déterminant et il existe des solutions adaptées à tous les types de climat, on peut avoir recours à des éléments textiles avec des membranes résistantes aux intempéries, dont les toiles de fibres de polyester ou de verre, sont recouvertes de téflon et tendues sur des piliers.

hotels
hoteles
hôtels
hotels

DER ENTWURF EINES HOTELS ist integral und spezialisiert und umfasst sowohl gemeinzugängliche, wie auch private Bereiche und der Erfolg des Hotels hängt sehr von deren wohlgelungener Verwirklichung ab. Auch die Außenräume sind entscheidend und es gibt Lösungen für alle Klimatypen. Eine für die Architektur interessante Alternative sind über Pfeiler gespannte, mit Teflon beschichtete, wetterbeständige Stoffmembranen aus Polyester- oder Glasfasern.

When the layout of the terrain is inclined or irregular, a multi-level design takes advantage of natural slopes. Constructing small, staggered buildings, aside from being a good solution, provides privacy for each space and makes each one an independent unit. When this option is combined with the use of locally produced materials exposed in their natural state, the harmonious relationship with the surrounding environment is enhanced, linking architecture and nature.

Cuando la configuración del terreno es inclinada o irregular hay que optar por un diseño en desniveles, en el que se aprovechen las pendientes naturales. La edificación de pequeñas construcciones escalonadas, además de convertirse en una buena solución, permite que cada espacio cuente con privacidad y sea independiente. Cuando a esta alternativa se le suma el uso de materiales que son producidos en el lugar y que son expuestos en su estado natural se fortalece la relación armónica con el entorno circundante, vinculando a la arquitectura con la naturaleza.

Lorsqu'un terrain est incliné ou irrégulier, il faut choisir un design en dénivelé, et profiter des pentes naturelles. L'utilisation de petites constructions en terrasses, permet que chaque espace ait une certaine intimité et soit indépendant. Lorsqu'à cette alternative on ajoute l'emploi de matériaux de la région à leur état naturel, on renforce son harmonie avec l'environnement, en mettant en relation l'architecture et la nature.

Bei schräger oder ungleichmäßiger Geländebeschaffenheit bietet sich der Entwurf mit verschiedenen Ebenen an, bei dem die natürlichen Hänge ausgenutzt werden. Das Errichten von kleinen gestuft angelegten Gebäuden wird nicht nur zur günstigen Lösung, sondern bietet auch jedem Raum Intimität und Unabhängigkeit. Wenn zu dieser Alternative noch die Anwendung von örtlich produzierten Materialien kommt, die in ihrem natürlichen Zustand gezeigt werden, dann stärkt das die harmonische Beziehung zur Umgebung, wodurch sich Architektur und Natur verbinden.

Curved roofs and arched walls are similar to the organic shapes found in nature, and thus are a sound design solution for spaces in natural ecosystems.

Las cubiertas curvas y los muros arqueados se asemejan a las formas orgánicas de la naturaleza, por lo que son una solución de diseño adecuada para espacios que se encuentran en ecosistemas naturales.

Les couronnements de murs courbes et les murs arqués se rapprochent des formes de la nature, et sont par conséquent des solutions adéquates pour des espaces situés dans des écosystèmes naturels.

Da sie den organischen Formen der Natur gleichen, sind gebogene Bedachungen und gewölbte Wände eine geeignete Lösung für den Entwurf von Räumen, die sich in natürlichen Ökosystemen befinden.

Ideally, areas for common use, located in places with warm weather where beautiful landscapes predominate, will be devised using schemes that have generous architectural openings or semi-openings toward the views enabling, to the extent possible, a fusion between interior and exterior, allowing for natural ventilation and thus creating a sensation of freedom.

Es ideal que las áreas de uso común, ya sean de estar, de comer o de convivencia, en lugares donde dominan los bellos paisajes y climas cálidos, se realicen bajo esquemas en los que se contemplen generosas aperturas o semi-aperturas arquitectónicas hacia las vistas, provocando la fusión entre interior y exterior, permitiendo la ventilación natural y creando una sensación de libertad.

Dans les climats chauds, pour mettre en valeur la vue des aires communes d'un hôtel, telles que salles à manger, de séjour ou de loisirs, on emploie de généreuses ouvertures ou semi ouvertures architecturales. On provoque ainsi une fusion entre l'intérieur et l'extérieur et on favorise aussi la ventilation naturelle en créant une sensation de liberté.

Für Gemeinschaftsräume zum Verbleiben, Essen oder Zusammentreffen, die sich dort befinden, wo schöne Landschaften dominieren und warmes Klima vorherrscht, ist ein Entwurf nach Schemen ideal, bei denen großzügige architektonische Öffnungen oder Halböffnungen zu diesen Ausblicken eingeplant werden, die das Verschmelzen zwischen Innen und Außen ermöglichen, das natürliche Lüftung bringt und ein Gefühl von Freiheit schafft.

Roofs made of leaves and branches from the region, as well as furniture made of hard fibers, are good architectural and decorative elements for use in warm weather.

Los techos realizados con hojas y ramas vegetales de la región así como los muebles hechos de fibras duras, también vegetales, son elementos arquitectónicos y decorativos adecuados para usar en climas cálidos.

Les toits de feuilles et de branches végétales originaires de la région et les meubles de fibres rigides, également végétales, sont des éléments architecturaux et décoratifs adéquats aux climats chauds.

Die Dächer aus Blättern und Zweigen der Pflanzen der Region, wie auch aus festen Pflanzenfasern gefertigte Möbel sind architektonische und dekorative Elemente, die für die Verwendung in heißem Klima geeignet sind.

If the exterior architecture of spaces on the seashore does not feature formal architectural divisions that interrupt or hinder the view of the landscape; if a modest scale is kept, in which architecture is not intended to be the protagonist of the space; and if decoration is discreet and, moreover, there is an attempt to link some of its elements and color with the environment, the focus of attention will be on the surrounding environment and there will be a feeling of peace and tranquility.

Si la solución de los espacios exteriores que se ubican frente al mar, no incluye divisiones formales que interrumpan o discontinúen la vista hacia el paisaje; si se guarda una escala modesta en la que no se pretenda hacer de la arquitectura la protagonista del espacio, y si la decoración es discreta e incluso se intenta que algunos de sus elementos y su colorido se relacionen con el ambiente, el foco de interés se centrará en el entorno circundante y se podrá generar una impresión de paz y tranquilidad.

Si l'architecture des espaces extérieurs en bord de mer ne comprend pas de divisions architecturales formelles qui interrompent la vue du paysage ; si l'on garde une échelle modeste dans laquelle on ne prétend pas faire de l'architecture le protagoniste de l'espace ; et si la décoration est discrète et qu'on essaie de lier des éléments et leurs couleurs à l'ambiance, le centre d'intérêt sera l'environnement et on pourra créer une impression de paix et de tranquillité.

Wenn die Architektur der am Meer liegenden Außenräume keine festen architektonischen Trennungen zeigt, die den Ausblick auf die Landschaft unterbrechen oder abbrechen; wenn der Maßstab bescheiden bleibt, da die Architektur nicht zum Hauptdarsteller des Raumes werden soll; und wenn die Innenausstattung sich diskret hält und es versucht wird, mit einigen Elementen und Farben einen Bezug zur Umwelt zu schaffen, dann konzentriert sich der Interessenbrennpunkt auf die Umgebung und ein Eindruck von friedlicher Ruhe kann erstehen.

The balanced repetition of some elements such as lounge chairs, sunshades, palm-roofed shades and even elements from natural vegetation gives the space rhythm.

La repetición equilibrada de algunos elementos como camastros, sombrillas, palapas e inclusive de la vegetación natural, concede al espacio un ritmo.

Pour imposer un rythme à un espace, on peut créer une répétition équilibrée : chaises longues, parasols, plantes, toits de feuilles de palme ou palapas.

Die ausgewogene Wiederholung von Elementen, wie Liegen, Schirme, pflanzliche Dächer und auch der natürlichen Pflanzenwelt, schenkt dem Raum Rhythmus.

offices   oficinas   bureaux   büroräume

TO A LARGE DEGREE, the decoration of the reception and waiting areas, as well as office conference rooms, expresses their image, and it is thus best that these spaces have interior planning that goes along with the intended message; however, whatever that message, the impression created must be one of order, something achieved using a few well-selected elements, such as furniture with simple lines and a limited range of colors.

LA DECORACIÓN de las zonas destinadas a recepción y espera, así como a salas de juntas de una oficina, expresa en buena medida la imagen de la misma, por lo que conviene que estos espacios cuenten con un interiorismo acorde con el mensaje que se desee externar; sin embargo, sea éste cual sea, la impresión siempre debe de ser de orden, cuestión que se logra con pocos y bien escogidos elementos, con mobiliario de líneas simples y recurriendo a una composición de colores limitada.

LA DÉCORATION de salles d'attente ou de réception et de salles de réunion d'un bureau expriment une image, c'est pourquoi il convient que ces espaces aient une décoration en accord avec le message que l'on cherche à transmettre ; cependant, l'impression doit toujours être un sentiment d'ordre, ce qui se réussit avec peu d'éléments bien choisis, avec un mobilier aux lignes simples et une composition de couleurs limitée.

DIE EINRICHTUNG von Empfangs- und Wartebereichen, so wie auch der Besprechungsräume einer Firma, ist wichtig für das Image derselben, weshalb diese Räume eine Innenausstattung vorweisen sollten, die die Botschaft weitergibt, die die Firma entsenden will. Allerdings muss immer der Eindruck von Ordnung geschaffen werden, was durch wenige vorsichtig gewählte Elemente, durch einfache Linien des Mobiliars und mittels der Wiederholung einer begrenzten Farbenkomposition bewirkt wird.

The use of transparent screens, openings and slots in interior design gives the impression of being in continuous and almost uninterrupted spaces.

El uso de transparencias, vanos y rendijas en el diseño interior favorece la impresión de estar en espacios continuos y apenas interrumpidos.

L'emploi de transparences, ouvertures et grilles dans la décoration d'intérieur augmente l'impression de continuité des espaces.

Das Verwenden von Transparenzen, Durchbrüchen und Gitterwerk beim Innenentwurf stärkt den Eindruck von kaum oder ununterbrochenen Räumen.

A clear lobby, free of architectural elements, has become the preferred choice both for rental and company-owned offices, due to the fact that it allows for a flexible use of space, subdividing areas using architectural or decorative elements and leaving the possibility of later rearrangement without great expense. Some of these elements may be glass, fabric screens or drywall, whether floor-to-ceiling or supported with light structures.

La planta libre, sin elementos arquitectónicos interpuestos, se ha convertido en la alternativa más frecuente tanto en las oficinas de renta como en las de compra; ello se debe a que permite aprovechar el espacio de una manera flexible, subdividiendo las áreas por medio de elementos arquitectónicos o decorativos y con la posibilidad de modificarlo posteriormente sin tener que realizar grandes gastos. Algunos de estos elementos pueden ser el vidrio, las transparencias de tela o los muros de tablarroca, ya sea de piso a techo o sostenidos con estructuras ligeras.

Les étages sans cloisons ou éléments architecturaux de division, sont devenus la structure la plus employée dans les bureaux, qu'ils soient propres ou de location. Cette solution permet de profiter d'un espace flexible, en sous divisant les aires au moyen d'éléments architecturaux ou décoratifs, avec la possibilité d'apporter des modifications sans trop de frais, on y emploie le verre, des tissus transparents, des cloisons de placoplâtre du sol au plafond ou soutenu par des structures légères.

Das freiräumige Stockwerk, ohne zwischengestellte architektonische Elemente, ist sowohl für gemietete, wie auch für gekaufte Büroräume zur meist gewählten Alternative geworden, weil es eine flexible Benutzung des Raumes ermöglicht, wobei die Bereiche durch architektonische oder dekorative Mittel unterteilt werden, was spätere Änderungen kostengünstig macht. Manche dieser Trennelemente sind aus Glas, aus Transparenzstoffen oder aus Gibskarton und gehen vom Fußboden bis zur Decke oder werden von leichten Strukturen gehalten.

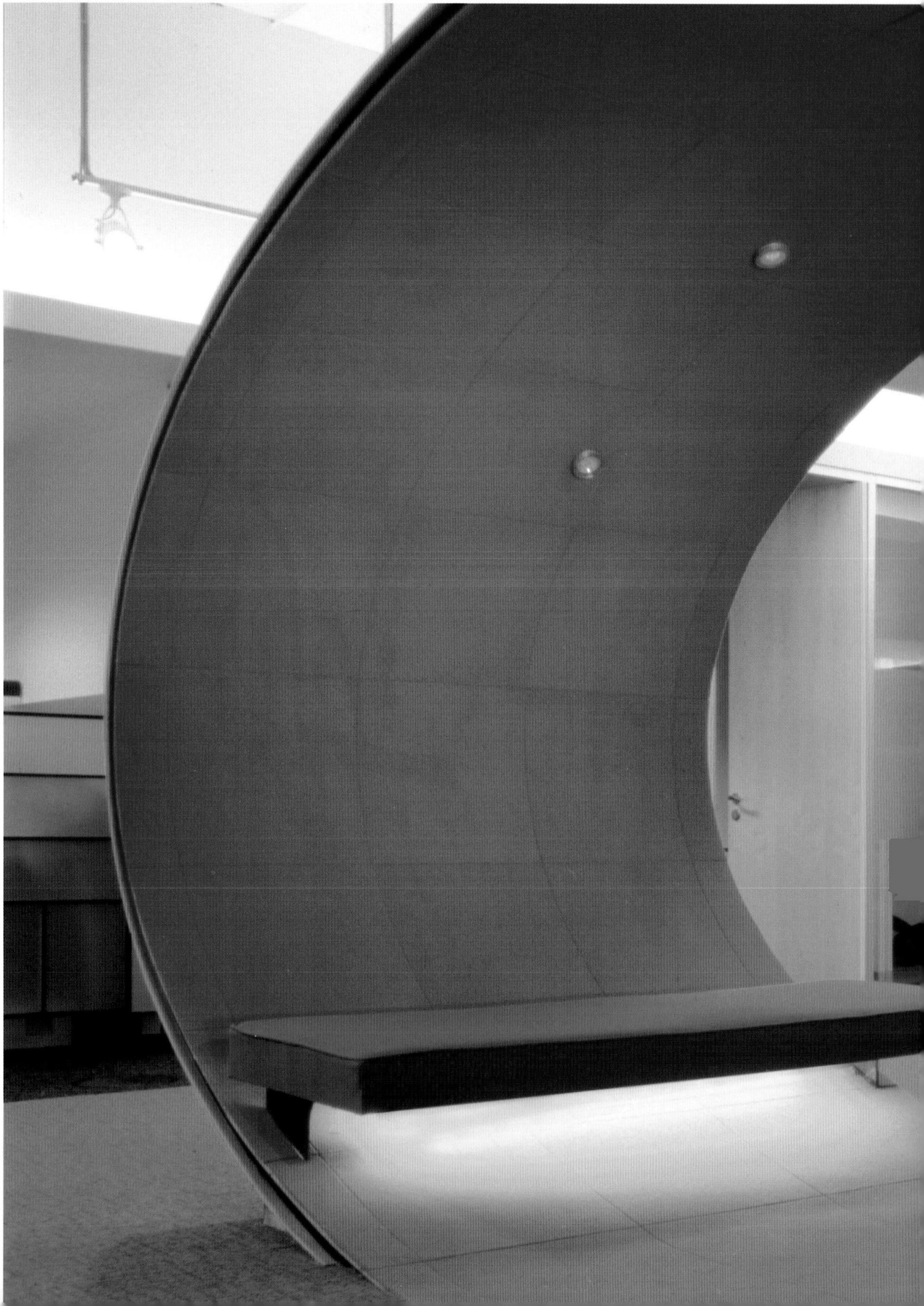

Mexikanska Telefón AB (AKTIEBOLAGET) L.M. Ericsson con el nombre en México de Empresa de Teléfonos Ericsson, S.A., conocida como Mexeric...

los postes y equipo de telefonía pública marcados con los color

ordenó que todos los beneficios de una red telefónica,

historia de la telefonía en México, pero logró salir adelante

al contar con el liderazgo de Gunnar Beckman, primero al frente de Ericsson

incorporación de todos los componentes dentro de una misma unidad.

conmutación AXE en Tlalnepantla y, cuatro años después comenzaría a exportarlas al ser designada esa planta como centro de producción para el Gru

Plentiful use of glass in the façades helps to keep interior and exterior spaces connected, and harnesses natural daylight to the highest possible extent.

El uso abundante del vidrio en las fachadas ayuda a que los espacios interiores y los exteriores permanezcan en contacto y a que se pueda aprovechar la luz natural del día al máximo.

L'emploi abondant du verre dans les façades contribue à mettre en contact les espaces intérieurs et extérieurs et permet de profiter au maximum de la lumière naturelle.

Die reichliche Verwendung von Glas in den Fassaden gestattet es den Innen- und Außenräumen in Verbindung zu stehen und erlaubt die größtmögliche Nutzung des natürlichen Tageslichtes.

Shafts are not only structural units able to support a load, but they can be part of the design and aesthetics of a building.

Las columnas no solamente se constituyen en unidades estructurales con capacidad de carga, sino que pueden formar parte del diseño y de la estética de una construcción.

Les piliers sont des unités structurelles avec capacité de charge et peuvent également contribuer au design et à l'esthétique d'une construction.

Stützpfeiler sind nicht nur strukturelle Einheiten mit Tragfähigkeit, sondern können auch zum Bestandteil des Entwurfes und der Ästhetik einer Bauwerkes werden.

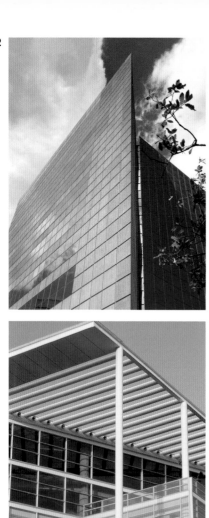

The evolution which has occurred in glass technology in terms of solar insulation, safety and self-cleaning has allowed for its use in architecture in large amounts and sizes, especially on façades, creating increasingly light and transparent buildings. Nonetheless, even with specialty glass, mullions and overhangs are needed to provide protection from the weather and to help reduce energy costs from the excessive use of air conditioning.

La evolución que ha habido en la tecnología del vidrio en términos del aislamiento solar, de seguridad y de autolimpieza, ha permitido su incorporación en grandes cantidades y dimensiones a la arquitectura, sobre todo a las fachadas, logrando construcciones cada vez más ligeras y transparentes. No obstante, aún cuando se trate de vidrios especiales se requiere de parteluces y volados que refuercen la protección climática y que ayuden a disminuir los gastos de energía por el uso inmoderado del aire acondicionado.

L'évolution de la technologie du verre en terme d'isolement thermique, de sécurité et nettoyage automatique a permis son incorporation en grandes quantités et dimensions à l'architecture, notamment aux façades, réalisant des constructions toujours plus légères et transparentes. Cependant, même s'il s'agit de verres spéciaux il est nécessaire d'installer des meneaux et dalles suspendues qui renforcent leur protection thermique et aident à diminuer les coûts dus à l'usage immodéré de la climatisation.

Die Entwicklung der Glastechnologie in Bezug auf Isolierung gegen Sonnenstrahlung, Sicherheit und Selbstsäuberung ermöglicht die Anwendung von Glas in großen Mengen und Maßen in der Architektur, vor allem in Fassaden, wodurch immer leichtere und durchsichtigere Bauwerke geschaffen werden. Trotzdem benötigt man auch bei Spezialglas noch Zwischenpfeiler und Auskragungen zum Verstärken des Klimaschutzes und um den Energieverbrauch zu reduzieren, der durch übermäßige Benutzung der Klimaanlagen entsteht.

Today, designers favor geometrically pure spaces, with a preference for capturing natural light and keeping a visual communication with the exterior; these values, combined with new translucent materials made with state-of-the-art technology, have facilitated better and more diverse solutions for architectural layout both in exteriors and interiors which enhance visual effects and allow for controlling the feeling of sharpness and size in the space.

Hoy en día existe una gran sensibilidad de los diseñadores hacia la creación de espacios geométricamente puros, de notoria expresión plástica, con preferencia por la captación de luz natural y que mantengan una comunicación visual con el exterior; estos valores, aunados a la aparición de nuevos materiales traslúcidos realizados con tecnología de vanguardia, han hecho posible que existan mejores y más diversas soluciones de composición arquitectónica, tanto en exteriores como en interiores, que se enriquezcan los efectos visuales y que se pueda controlar la sensación de amplitud y nitidez del espacio.

Dernièrement, les designers montrent une grande sensibilité à la création d'espaces géométriquement purs, à une expression plastique notoire, avec une préférence pour la captation de lumière naturelle qui maintient une communication visuelle avec l'extérieur. Ces valeurs, unies à l'apparition de nouveaux matériaux translucides de technologies de pointe, ont rendu possible l'existence de meilleures solutions, de compositions architecturales plus variées, pour l'extérieur comme l'intérieur, qui enrichissent les effets visuels et qui contrôlent la sensation d'amplitude et de pureté de l'espace.

Heutzutage existiert beim Design eine große Empfindsamkeit zur Schöpfung von geometrisch reinen Räumen mit notorisch plastischem Ausdruck, die dank der Vorliebe für die Nutzung von natürlichem Licht, eine visuelle Verbindung mit Außen erhalten. Diese Vorzüge, zusammen mit dem Auftreten neuer lichtdurchlässiger Materialien durch Spitzentechnologie, ermöglichen die Existenz von besseren und vielfältigen Lösungen für die architektonische Komposition, sowohl für Außen, wie auch für Innen, die Bereicherung der visuellen Effekte und das kontrollierte Erwecken eines Gefühls von räumlicher Weite und Reinheit.

If there is a trademark of modern offices, it is the tendency to use functional, lasting furniture that provides sufficient storage space and comfort.

Si por algo se distingue la oficina actual es por la inclinación hacia el uso de mobiliario funcional, que sea durable, que cuente con sitio suficiente de guardado y que ofrezca comodidad.

Les bureaux actuels se différencient par un penchant pour le mobilier fonctionnel, qui soit durable, avec les rangements et le confort nécessaires.

Wenn moderne Büroräume sich durch etwas hervorheben, ist das die Neigung zur Verwendung von funktionellem Mobiliar, das haltbar ist, genug Ablageraum hat und Bequemlichkeit bietet.

Some horizontal elements, such as bridges between spaces, create a more kind and human perception of architecture.

Algunos elementos horizontales, como es el caso de los puentes que comunican un espacio con otro, permiten que la escala de la arquitectura se perciba más amable y humana.

Certains éléments horizontaux, comme les ponts qui communiquent un espace à un autre, permettent que l'architecture soit perçue de manière plus agréable et humaine.

Einige horizontale Elemente, wie etwa Brücken, die Räume miteinander verbinden, erlauben eine zuvorkommende und menschlichere Wahrnehmung des architektonischen Maßstabs.

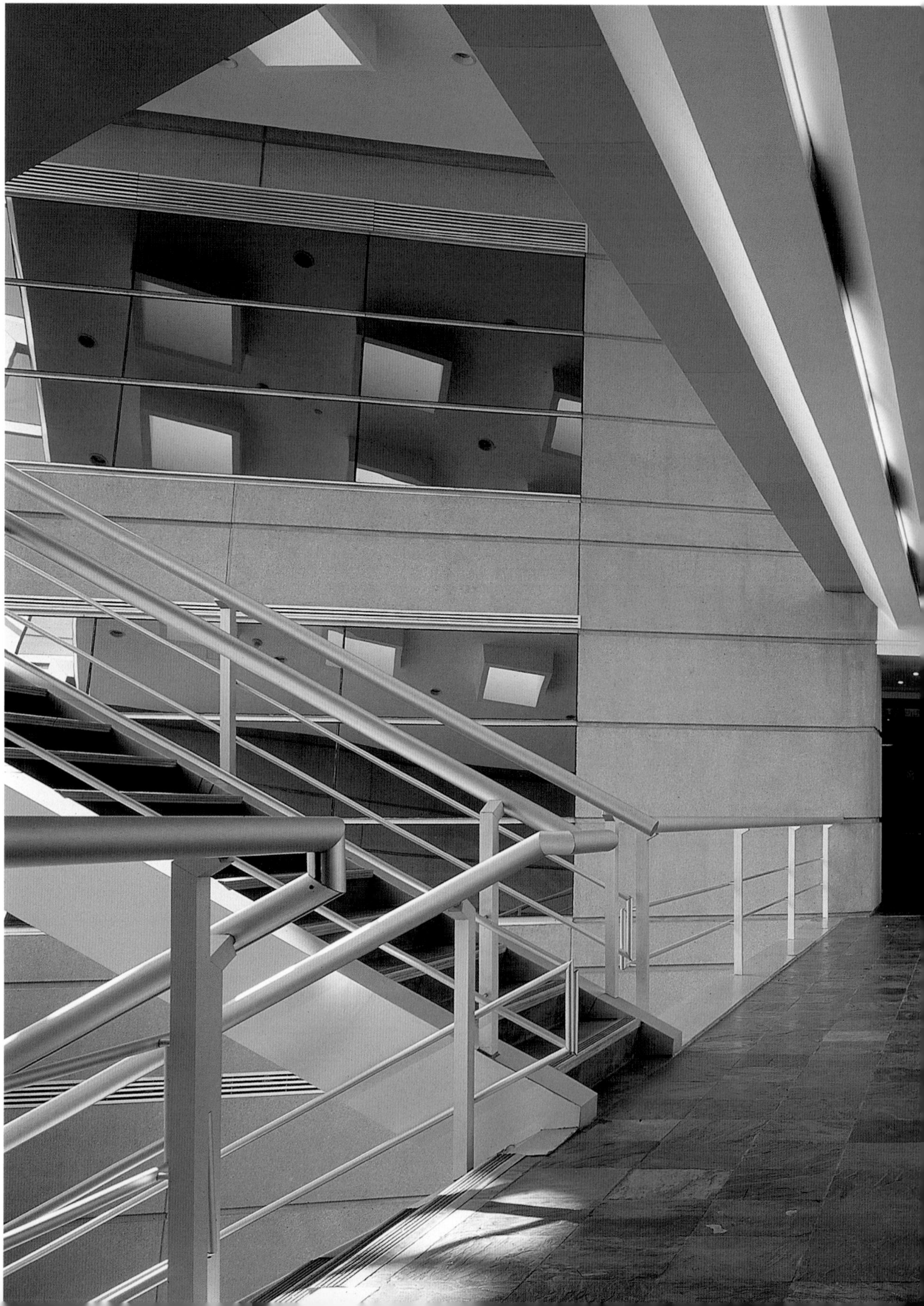

Owing to their extensive possibilities for use, color variety, texture and finishes, aesthetic quality and lifespan, both wood and leather furniture continue to have a strong presence in the design of interior workspaces; it is best, however, to combine them with other materials and finishes with considerably lighter tones.

Gracias a sus multiples posibilidades de aplicación, a su variedad de color, texturas y acabados, a su calidad estética y a su duración, tanto la madera como los muebles de piel siguen teniendo una fuerte presencia en el diseño de espacios interiores de trabajo; conviene, sin embargo, combinarlos con otros materiales y acabados cuyas tonalidades sean considerablemente más claras.

Le bois et les meubles en cuir ont encore une forte
présence dans le design des bureaux, grâce à leurs
nombreuses possibilités d'application, leur variété de
couleurs, de textures et finitions, leur qualité esthétique
et leur durée de vie ; il convient, cependant, de les
mélanger avec d'autres matériaux et finitions avec des
tonalités plus claires.

Dank ihrer weitreichenden Anwendungsmöglichkeiten, ihrer
Farbvielfalt, Texturen und Endbehandlungen, ihrer ästhetischen
Qualität und Haltbarkeit zeigen das Holz und die Ledermöbel
auch weiterhin eine starke Gegenwart beim Entwurf von
inneren Arbeitsräumen. Trotzdem empfiehlt es sich, sie mit
anderen Materialien und Oberflächen in bedeutend helleren
Töne zu kombinieren.

THE RESTAURANT BUSINESS is currently among the sectors with greatest development, where the quality and refinement of food go hand-in-hand with the originality of a building. Tensile architecture that uses membranes in interior spaces is an innovative resource, as its use is most commonly associated with exteriors. These tensile structures may work in interior spaces as lattices, sometimes being walls or ceilings, using fabrics and decorative poles to stretch them.

EL NEGOCIO DE RESTAURANTES es en la actualidad uno de los rubros comerciales con mayor desarrollo, donde la calidad y el refinamiento de la comida van de la mano con la originalidad de un edificio. La arquitectura textil de membranas en interiores es un recurso innovador, pues su uso se asocia mayormente con exteriores. Estas tensoestructuras pueden actuar en los espacios interiores como cerramientos haciendo as veces de muros o de techos, utilizando telas y postes decorativos para tensarlas.

L'HOTELLERIE EST ACTUELLEMENT l'une des activités commerciales avec le plus de croissance, où la qualité et le raffinement de la cuisine se donnent a main avec l'originalité de la construction. L'emploi de membranes extiles dans les intérieurs est une ressource innovante, puisqu'elles sont principalement associées aux extérieurs. Ces structures peuvent s'utiliser dans les espaces intérieurs comme fermetures remplaçant murs ou toits, en utilisant des tissus et des piliers décoratifs pour les tendre.

DER RESTAURANTBETRIEB ist heutzutage einer der sich meist entwickelnden Gewerbezweige, wo Qualität und Raffinesse der Gerichte mit der Originalität eines Gebäudes Hand in Hand gehen. Die textile Architektur der Membranen in Innenräumen ist eine innovative Ressource, weil ihre Verwendung sich sonst hauptsächlich auf Außenräume bezieht. Diese ensostrukturen können in Innenräumen so eingesetzt werden, dass sie zugleich als Wände und Decken dienen, indem man Stoffe benutzt und dekorative Pfeiler, um sie zu spannen.

varied spaces
espacios diversos
espaces divers
allerlei räume

There are solutions for architectural and decorative divisions of space whose importance doesn't necessarily lie in their size, but rather in the way they break up walkways or in their visual role in the space; some examples are: water surfaces, long storage furniture, bridges, translucent screens, slots, handrails, fountains, flower-boxes and even a different material from that used for the floor.

Existen soluciones arquitectónicas y decorativas para dividir el espacio cuya importancia no necesariamente radica en sus dimensiones, sino en la manera en que interrumpen las circulaciones o en el peso visual que tienen en el conjunto, algunos ejemplos de ellas son: espejos de agua, muebles largos de guardado, puentes, mamparas transparentes, rejillas, barandales, fuentes, jardineras e inclusive la inserción de un material distinto al que domina en los pisos.

Il existe des solutions architecturales et décoratives
pour diviser l'espace dont l'importance ne réside pas
nécessairement dans ses dimensions mais dans la manière
dont ils interrompent la circulation ou dans leur poids
visuel dans l'espace comme les miroirs d'eau, meubles
longs de rangement, ponts, cloisons transparentes, grilles,
balustrades, fontaines, jardinières, ou à l'emploi d'un
matériau différent à celui qui domine les sols.

Beispiele architektonischer und dekorativer Raumtrennungen,
die nicht unbedingt wegen ihrer Maßen wichtig sind,
sondern wegen ihrer Art den Verkehr zu unterbrechen und
wegen dem visuellen Gewicht, das sie im Raum einnehmen:
spiegelnde Wasseroberflächen, große Schrankmöbel, Brücken,
Wandschirme, Transparenzstrukturen, Gitter, Geländer,
Springbrunnen, Blumenkästen und auch ein Material, das
anders ist, als das in den Böden dominierende.

Dining companions enjoy, when circumstances allow, being out in the open air; and so restaurants and cafes have conquered space by using terraces, sometimes at ground level, and sometimes on the higher levels of buildings, or else by taking over sidewalks and thus generating a unique urban concept where landscape design and the inclusion of shade-providing elements is particularly important; although for properly using the latter it is best that the atmosphere is informal.

A los comensales les gusta, en tanto las circunstancias lo permitan, estar al aire libre; por ello los restaurantes y cafés han ganado espacio a través de terrazas, unas veces en la planta baja y otras en los niveles superiores, o bien extendiéndose hacia las banquetas y generando un concepto urbano particular donde el diseño de paisaje y la inclusión de elementos que brindan sombra tienen especial importancia; aunque estos últimos deben ser resueltos adecuadamente, conviene que el ambiente que se cree sea informal.

Lorsque les circonstances le permettent, la clientèle des restaurants préfère rester à l'air libre; c'est pourquoi les restaurants et cafés ont gagné de l'espace grâce à des terrasses qui sont parfois au rez-de-chaussée, dans les niveaux supérieurs des constructions ou s'étendent vers les trottoirs et génèrent un concept urbain particulier où le design du paysage et les parasols ou autres éléments de même fonction ont une importance particulière ; bien que ces derniers doivent être bien pensés, il est préférable que l'ambiance créée soit informelle.

Die Gäste ziehen es vor, wenn immer möglich, an der freien Luft zu verweilen, weshalb Restaurants und Cafés durch Terrassen Platz gewonnen haben, die sich manchmal im Erdgeschoss oder sonst in den oberen Stockwerken der Gebäude befinden oder sich zu den Bürgersteigen hin ausbreiten und ein spezielles städtisches Konzept schaffen, bei dem die Landschaftsgestaltung und das Einbeziehen von schattenspendenden Elementen äußerst wichtig sind, allerdings sollte, zum angemessenen Schöpfen dieser Letzteren, das Ambiente eher ungezwungen sein.

Wood beams, iron finishes, simulated stone, brick and concrete, aluminum, metha-crylates or stainless steel pieces are structural elements and building materials that, when exposed in their natural state as part of interior decoration, determine the color palette of the ambiance and create specific atmospheres that evoke similarities with industrial premises or old country haciendas. Some of them evoke cold ambiances, and others warmth, so it is best to combine them with other materials.

Las vigas de madera, los acabados de hierro, la piedra, el ladrillo y el concreto aparente, los aluminios, los metacrilatos o las piezas de acero inoxidable, son elementos estructurales y materiales constructivos que cuando son expuestos en su forma natural y a la vista como parte de la decoración de interiores, determinan el colorido del ambiente y componen atmósferas particulares que recuerdan las construcciones industriales o antiguas haciendas campiranas. Algunos de ellos evocan ambientes fríos y otros cálidos, por lo que es preferible su mezcla con otros materiales.

Afin de composer des atmosphères particulières qui rapprochent les constructions industrielles des anciennes haciendas, on peut employer les éléments structurels et matériaux de construction apparents suivants, à leur état naturel : poutres en bois, finitions de fer, pierre, brique et ciment apparents, aluminiums, méthacrylates ou pièces d'acier inoxydable. Certains évoquent des ambiances froides et d'autres chaleureuses, c'est pourquoi il convient de mélanger les matériaux entre eux.

Die sichtbaren Holzbalken, das Schmiedeeiserne, die Natur- und Ziegelsteine und der Beton, das Aluminium, die Metacrylate oder die Edelstahlteile sind strukturelle Elemente und Baustoffe, die den Farbton des Ambiente bestimmen, wenn sie in ihrer natürlichen Form, als Bestandteile der Innenausstattung zu sehen sind und sie schaffen spezielle Atmosphären, die an industrielle Bauwerke erinnern lassen oder an manche alte Herrschaftssitze auf dem Land. Einige schöpfen kühle Ambiente und andere gemütliche, weshalb es sich empfiehlt Materialien zu mischen.

In spaces with high ceilings, horizontal elements such as window sills, the height of furniture and lamps, paintings, among others, allow the scale to become more human.

En espacios donde los techos son muy altos, elementos horizontales como los perfiles de las ventanas, la altura de los muebles y lámparas, los cuadros, entre otros, permiten que la escala se convierta en más humana.

Dans des espaces où les toits sont très hauts, les éléments horizontaux comme les cadres des fenêtres, la hauteur des meubles et des lampes ou les tableaux, entre autres, permettent que l'échelle devienne plus humaine.

In Räumen mit sehr hohen Zimmerdecken ermöglichen es horizontale Elemente, wie etwa Gemälde, Fensterprofile und die Höhe von Mobiliar und Lampen, den Maßstab menschenfreundlicher erscheinen zu lassen.

apartments departamentos appartements wohnungen

Durability and lightness are increasingly compatible concepts due to technological progress in the production of glass and steel; nowadays both materials may work structurally and ornamentally in a building, enabling the architectural work to gain a unique lightness and letting it become a glass box that allows for the entrance of light during the day and becomes a source for it at night. These luminous effects are enhanced when perforated galvanized steel sheets are also used.

Resistencia y ligereza, son conceptos cada vez más compatibles gracias a los avances tecnológicos en la producción del vidrio y del acero; hoy en día, ambos materiales pueden trabajar en una construcción, tanto de forma estructural como decorativa, permitiendo que la obra arquitectónica adquiera una liviandad única y que se pueda convertir en una caja de vidrio, que durante el día facilite la penetración de la luz y por la noche se constituya en su emisora. Estos efectos luminosos se enriquecen cuando se usan además láminas de acero galvanizado perforadas.

Résistance et légèreté sont des concepts de plus en plus compatibles grâce aux avancements technologiques nés de la production du verre et de l'acier. Aujourd'hui les deux matériaux peuvent travailler dans une construction, dans sa structure et décoration, donnant une légèreté unique à l'oeuvre architecturale et pouvant la convertir en une cage de verre qui facilite la pénétration de la lumière le jour et qui émette cette dernière la nuit. Ces effets lumineux s'enrichissent en ajoutant des plaques d'acier galvanisé perforées.

Beständigkeit und weniger Gewicht sind, dank der technologischen Fortschritte in der Glas- und Stahlherstellung, immer besser zu kombinierende Konzepte. Heutzutage können beide Stoffe in einem Gebäude strukturell und dekorativ verwendet werden, womit das architektonische Werk eine einzigartige Leichtigkeit erhält und sich in einen Glaskasten verwandelt, der tagsüber dem Licht das Eindringen vereinfacht und nachts zum Ausstrahler desselben wird. Diese Leuchteffekte werden bereichert, wenn man außerdem noch gelöcherte feuerverzinkte Stahlbleche benutzt.

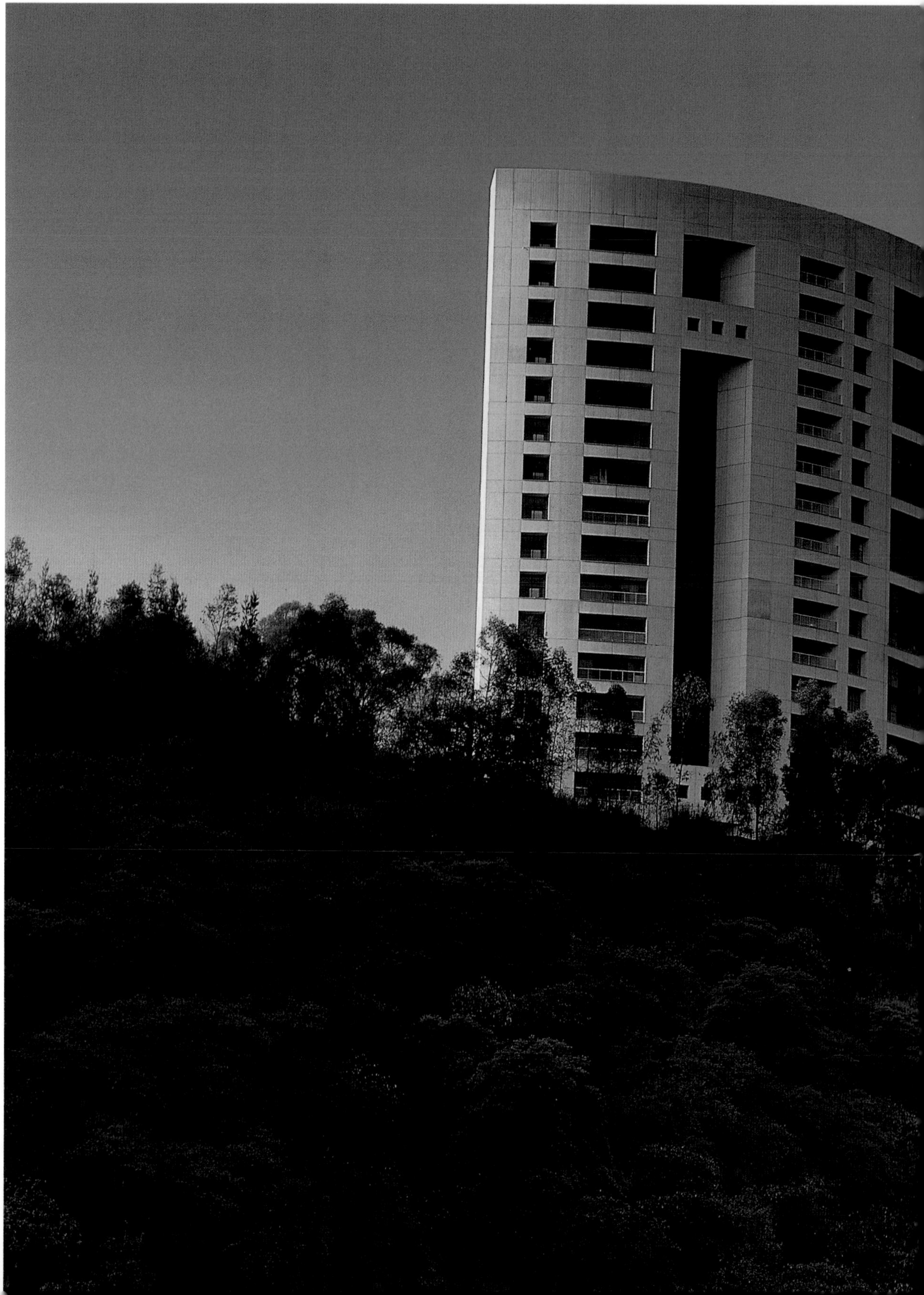

Concrete and glass are materials that facilitate a different layout and manipulation of volume in a building; while the former evokes warmth, it is rugged and blocks the entrance of light; the latter conveys a feeling of lightness, it is sleek, and its transparency lets light in; one is the quintessential material for solid spaces, the other is conceived as the ideal covering for certain openings. Harnessing and bringing out the properties of the materials becomes an essential tool for the designer.

El concreto y el vidrio son materiales que permiten concebir y manipular de distinta manera los volúmenes de una construcción; mientras el primero evoca solidez, es rugoso y evita el paso de la luz, el segundo da la sensación de ligereza, es liso y su transparencia permite que traspase la luminosidad; en tanto que uno es el material por excelencia para los macizos, el otro es concebido como ideal para cubrir algunos vanos. Aprovechar y exaltar las propiedades de los materiales se constituye en una herramienta esencial para el diseñador.

Le ciment et le verre sont des matériaux qui permettent de concevoir et manipuler différemment les volumes d'une construction; alors que le premier est rugueux, évoque la solidité et évite le passage de la lumière, le second est lisse, donne une sensation de légèreté et sa transparence laisse passer la luminosité ; si bien que l'un est le matériel par excellence pour les éléments massifs, et que l'autre sert à couvrir les ouvertures. Profiter des propriétés des matériaux et les amplifier font parti des outils essentiels de l'architecte.

Beton und Glas sind Stoffe, die es ermöglichen die Rauminhalte eines Bauwerkes auf verschiedene Weisen zu entwerfen und zu manipulieren. Während der rauhe Beton Festigkeit bietet und kein Licht durchlässt, erweckt glattes Glas das Gefühl von Leichtigkeit und seine Transparenz erlaubt den Lichteinfall. Damit ist Beton ein hervorragendes Material für festes Mauerwerk und Glas dient beim Entwurf als ideale Füllung von Öffnungen. Die Eigenschaften der Materialien zu nutzen und hervorzuheben ist ein wesentliches Instrument des Designs.

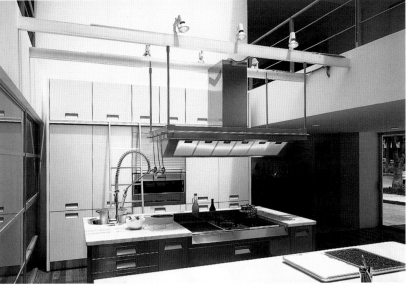

architectonic
arquitectónicos
architectoniques
architektonische

photographic
fotográficos
photographiques
fotografische

alfonso de béjar • pgs. 10 (right), 186 a 191, 192 (top), 260-261.

alberto moreno • pgs. 209 (bottom), 222 (center).

antonio pavón • pgs. 7 (center), 54, 76-77, 80 (top), 150 (left), 151 (right), 184-185, 211 a 215.

basilisco editores • pgs. 192-293 (bottom), 193 (top).

denisse escamilla • pgs. 77 (right), 144 (top), 200 (bottom), 201 (top).

fernando cordero • pgs. 7 (left), 8, 66, 68-69, 84 (left), 98 (top), 100-101, 111 a 115, 124-125, 126, 130, 139, 144-145 (bottom), 145 (top), 208 (bottom), 216 a 221.

geno perches • pg. 252.

guillermo soto • pg. 90-91.

héctor velasco facio • pgs. 3, 6, 7 (right), 9, 14-15, 17 a 20, 24-25, 62-63, 67, 102-103, 106 a 109, 116 (top left and right), 118-119, 120 a 123, 127, 128 (left), 129 (right), 133 a 135, 141 (bottom), 146 (left), 146-147 (right), 172 a 175, 235, 238-239.

henry fechtman • pg. 201 (bottom).

ignacio urquiza • pgs. 204-205, 207, 209 (top), 230-231.

jaime navarro • pgs. 132 (center), 222 (bottom center).

jordi farré • pgs. 27, 40-43, 46-47, 177 (bottom), 250-251.

jorge ávila • pgs. 11 (right), 210, 228-229.

jorge taboada • pgs. 78-79, 80 (bottom), 81 a 83, 116 (bottom).

lourdes legorreta • pgs. 46 (left), 47 (right), 55, 73, 80 (center).

luis gordoa • pgs. 11 (left), 60, 105, 155, 157, 160-161, 164 a 167, 168 (top), 169 (top), 170-171, 182-183, 208 (top right), 222 (top left, top right and bottom right), 240 a 243, 246 a 249, 254 a 257, 262-263.

maría moreno • pg. 140 (top left).

mary nichols • pgs. 194 (bottom), 197.

michael calderwood • pgs. 21 a 23, 28 a 31, 34-39, 198-199, 200 (top), 222 (center left), 223, 258-259,

paul czitrom • pgs. 4-5, 53 (right), 58 (top right), 59 (top), 92 a 95, 148-149, 152 a 154, 158-159, 180-181, 222 (bottom left), 224-225, 226 (left), 227 (right), 270-271.

ricardo morales gonzález • pgs. 177 (top), 178-179.

sandra pereznieto • pgs. 58 (top left and bottom), 59 (bottom), 74-75, 132 (top and bottom), 208 (top left).

sebastián saldívar • pgs. 32-33, 44-45, 56-57, 64-65, 84 (top right and bottom), 86-87, 96-97, 128-129, 131, 136-137, 140 (bottom), 222 (top center and center right), 244-245.

susan goines • pgs. 194 (top), 195, 202-203.

tania zacarías • pgs. 49 a 51, 70-71.

werner huthmacher • pgs. 10 (left), 150-151, 226-227, 232, 233, 236-237.

victor benitez • pg. 141 (top).